THE HALL OF THE MOUNTAIN KING

A BOY MEETS ROCK LOVE STORY

AFTER HENRIK IBSEN'S "PEER GYNT"

HENRI RENNIE

The Hall Of The Mountain King

Copyright © 2024 by Henri Rennie

All rights reserved.

Print ISBN: 978-0-6454050-6-4

E-book ISBN: 978-0-6454050-7-1

Published by **Meredian Creative 2024**

Ballina, Australia

No part of this book may be reproduced in any form or by any electronic or mechanical means, including information storage and retrieval systems, without written permission from the author, except for the use of brief quotations in a book review.

No performance without written permission from Meredian Creative. Please direct all enquiries to www.meredian.com.au

 Created with Vellum

In fond and respectful memory of Brian Cannon - teacher, director, mentor and friend.

And for my Muse - my darling bride Meredith.

CONTENTS

DRAMATIS PERSONAE	vii
First production	ix
ACT 1, Scene 1	1
ACT 1, Scene 2	9
ACT 1, Scene 3	22
ACT 1, Scene 4	35
ACT 1, Scene 5	46
Photographs	75
ACT 2, Scene 1	77
ACT 2, Scene 2	83
ACT 2, Scene 3	92
ACT 2, Scene 4	100
ACT 2, Scene 5	121
ACT 2, Scene 6	145
From the Playwright...	159
NOTES for Directors	161
Also by Henri 'Renoir' Rennie	163

DRAMATIS PERSONAE

PEER GYNT – son of a peasant, with grand ideas, and an aversion to commitment.

CHALKIE – a white-faced troll who can mix in human society if he chooses to.

CHRYSOPRASE (CHRYSSIE) – green daughter of the troll king, used to having her own way.

FERROUS – red king of the trolls, old and traditionally minded.

CITRINE - Ferrous' yellow grandmother, deaf and seemingly dotty.

SANDY – Chryssie's attendant, sweet and innocent by troll standards, at least. Orange/tan, could pass for a human who's been in the sun a lot.

ROSE, SMOKIE and AMY – the king's three sisters, pink, brown and purple respectively, argumentative and sometimes blood-thirsty, but believe they're the real power behind the throne, know all the traditions but less bound to them than the king.

CLIFF – large grey troll who sometimes acts as the king's 'muscle'.

BOULDER – son of Peer & Chryssie, human-skinned with patches of green, has the worst features of both parents. Should be played by the same actor as plays PEER.

* *Trolls' skin and clothes reflect the colour of their particular stone. Hair not necessarily so. They are tattooed on one side of the face, although CHALKIE's is obscured by powder when 'outside'. For the first production, these tattoos were based on old Anglo-Saxon runes. The KING's rune was then used as a motif on wall hangings in the hall itself.*

THE HALL OF THE MOUNTAIN KING was first presented by the Lismore Theatre Company in Goonellabah, New South Wales, in May 2025 with the following cast:

    PEER/BOULDER................Maitraya Stewart
    CHALKIE............................Graham Andrews
    CHRYSSIE.......................................Jenni Law
    SANDY.....................Audrey O'Donnell-Parr
    CLIFF......................Morgan Montague-Elliott
    ROSE..Shae Salmon
    SMOKIE...................................Lola Crawley
    AMY...Jenny Craig
    CITRINE..................................Sylvia Clarke
    KING FERROUS...........................Brian Fry

The play was directed by Henri Rennie
with Jos Wright.
Stage management by Erika Dansie.
Costumes by Jess Laughton.
Lights and sound by Oliver Britt and Steve Nossiter.

ACT 1, SCENE 1

1:1

(MUSIC: *Greig's "Hall of the Mountain King". Fade down.*
   Lights up: A bar in Henriksberg - 'Rick's' sign visible, perhaps as a projection.
   CHALKIE stands drinking a vodka. PEER enters holding a drink (Stone & Wood?), looking over his shoulder nervously.
   "Rock Around The Clock" plays in the background, gradually fading out.)

PEER: Thanks, Rick. Oh! Chalkie?

CHALKIE: Peer.

. . .

PEER: What are you doing here?

CHALKIE: Enjoying a quiet vodka.

PEER: Weren't you invited to the wedding? I thought the whole village was going!

CHALKIE: I believe so, yes. I'll get there, just fashionably late. I'm not keen on hanging around and mingling with people. I don't like crowds of – er... I don't like crowds. What about you? I thought Moe and Ingrid had invited the whole village. Barring essential services, like Rick's. *(Raises glass)*

PEER: I suppose Rick has to set up here, ready for the reception.

CHALKIE: The post-game show.

PEER: Yeah. And I am invited, yes. Just, um, have a bit of a problem. *(Looks unhappily at his mobile phone)* Can you keep a secret?

CHALKIE: Better than you can possibly imagine.

PEER: Oh, you'd be surprised what I can imagine. I got a message from Ingrid this morning. I think she's expecting that I'll run off with her at the absolute last minute. Save her from a life with Moe, who she's realised is the most miserable bloke in the village.

. . .

CHALKIE: Where would she get that idea? Oh. From you.

PEER: Well, I might have proposed something to that effect. When I say 'proposed', I don't mean actually *proposed*. Just sort of, tossed out the idea, as it were.

CHALKIE: I see. So, she expects you to have turned up on your white charger and...

PEER: I don't have a white Charger. I don't have *any* sort of car, in *any* colour. Actually, I don't even have a licence.

CHALKIE: Greyhound?

PEER: Not even a dog licence.

CHALKIE: I meant a bus, Peer. Go off with her on a bus. I saw that in a movie, once.

PEER: Chalkie, it's Sunday in Henriksberg. There's no such thing as public transport. Little enough at the best of times, but today? No chance. No buses. No trains, although there's been a rail service, light or otherwise, promised for up here at every election as far back as my mother can remember, and she's really old.

CHALKIE: Yes, so they have. At least they've been consistent.

. . .

PEER: And the only taxi in town belongs to Ingrid's Dad.

CHALKIE: Tricky, yes, I can see that. So, what will you do?

PEER: For a start, I can say I didn't get her message. That would be plausible. The phone service in Henriksberg is notoriously bad.

CHALKIE: I don't think that's quite accurate.

PEER: You don't think it's bad?

CHALKIE: I don't think it's a service. But still, it *is* better than what you get once you get up into the hills, believe me. It's another world up there, and phone service is not a happening thing. So, you'll just leave the bride standing at the altar? With her groom.

PEER: What else can I do? I wasn't serious. I was just – consoling her. Indulging a bit of fantasy.

CHALKIE: Hers, or yours?

PEER: Oh, hers. Mine was, well, already being indulged at the time. A bit.

CHALKIE: Mm. *(Nods.)* Peer, if you *are* going to do a runner, or at least a walker, don't you think that you'd be better off getting as good a head start as you can, rather than stopping for a drink before you even begin?

PEER: I know, I know. I *should*. I guess I just don't have any idea of where to go.

CHALKIE: When you don't know where you're going, it doesn't matter what direction you go in, I read that somewhere.

PEER: Wise words. But not helping.

CHALKIE: Sorry. *(Both drink in silence.)*

PEER: The hills! You mentioned the hills – I could go up there. Keep away from the main road. The main road's the first place they'll look for me.

CHALKIE: You think they'll come looking for you?

PEER: Ingrid will. Probably the whole village, if she makes a big enough scene.

CHALKIE: Is that likely?

PEER: Have you *met* Ingrid?

. . .

CHALKIE: Only in passing.

PEER: Best way to do it. Certainly, passing is what I should have done. Chalkie, what's on the other side of the hills up there? I haven't travelled much that way. Wandered about a bit, but not really travelled, you understand?

CHALKIE: On the other side? More hills. Mountains, if you go far enough. If you go far enough, eventually you'll see the sea. That's true of anywhere, I suppose, if you're persistent enough.

PEER: The sea? That would be... a change. Otherwise, it's downhill right from the outset. Y'know, Chalkie, I don't like the sound of that. Start as you mean to continue, I say! Onward and upward.

CHALKIE: Up, up and away? That's something to aspire to.

PEER: Maybe not that far. But yes, certainly, away. To the hills. I'll stop in at Mum's, pick up some clothes and things – she'll already be at the church, like most everyone else in the village. Yes! That's the plan!

CHALKIE: *(slowly)* I, er, have... family, up in the hills.

PEER: Will you come with me? As soon as we finish these drinks...

. . .

CHALKIE: No. After this drink, I'll go to the wedding, and be seen. If we were to both vanish together, at the same time, it might give some people ideas.

PEER: What? That you and I...? That's crazy! We play darts together at the pub, that's all. I mean, we're *mates* I guess, but...

CHALKIE: You know that, and I know that. But Henriksberg is a small place.

PEER: Full of small people, with small minds. You're right. I'm better than that. *We're* better than that, but *they*'d never let the truth get in the way of a good story.

CHALKIE: No, *they* wouldn't, would they?

PEER: Right, I'll head for the hills. Where should I look for your family?

CHALKIE: You shouldn't. If any of them want to find you, they will. But I suggest that you really try to be self-sufficient.

PEER: Sufficient unto myself, eh? Good thinking, Chalkie. I can live off the land, I'm sure.

CHALKIE: *(quietly)* Just make sure it doesn't live off you. *(To PEER)* Something like that, yes.

. . .

PEER: You've inspired me, old man. I'm off! *(downs his drink at a gulp, and exits.)*

CHALKIE: I sometimes think you really are, Peer. When the going gets tough, that's tough, you're going. What's annoying is that you're otherwise a likeable sort of chap. Certainly, more interesting than anyone else that I've encountered in this village, which isn't difficult. Most of the men are duller than the back edge of an axe, and most of the women sparkle like hessian sacks. *(Shakes his head sadly.)* Their only saving grace is that at least they're a change from my own lot. A different set of dullards. I sometimes think I should travel further afield. Experience places and things that I've read about here. Reading – hah! That alone puts me ahead of most of mine. What they know about the world at large could be written on a river stone, and still leave room for three verses of a saga. *(Sips and sighs.)* Oh, Peer, you daft sod – if you <u>do</u> actually head for the hills, keep your head down and keep going until you reach the other side. Any decent troll would squash you like a frog, assuming there was such a thing as a decent troll. Present company excepted. *(Stares into his glass.)*

BLACKOUT

(Music fragment: "Here we are and here we go - Rocking All Over The World")

ACT 1, SCENE 2

1 :2

(THE WOODS *(dappled green light FX).*
Music fragment: "Rocky Mountain Way".
Wild bird noises, and the sound of crashing through shrubbery, with appropriate cursing and swearing. More bird noises.
PEER enters, staggering and panting, his shirt and trousers torn and grubby.)

PEER: They're all after me now – I'm sure of it! The whole bloody village. The whole wretched parish, I'll bet! Oh, I shouldn't have snuck down to see just how much fuss I'd actually caused, but, I wanted to see who cared.

About me, nobody. Of course. But Ingrid and her parents – God, what a fuss! You'd think nobody knew what the girl was like before she pitched her fit on the way to the altar! Wailing about her disappointment – I mean, it's not my fault if Moe doesn't measure up, is it?

(Stops for breath, and examines his tattered clothes) I do wish Mum had been a bit more up-to-date with the laundry. Some clean clothes would have been nice. I suppose I could have taken the wedding outfit she'd laid out for me, but I really don't want to be reminded of the whole Ingrid business. Talk about dodging a bullet. Commitment, *(shakes his head)* being 'committed' is when they lock you in an institution, and they do say marriage is an institution. Imagine – a life sentence for moment's fun. A moment or two.

No looking back, Peer! Chin up, best foot forward, seize the day and all that stuff! This is the start of a whole new life for me! A new life, where I can be whatever, or whoever, I want to be! *(Stops again, satisfied all is quiet, he sits down, near front of stage.)*

No sound of pursuit. I must have outrun them all. Hah – of course! There's none among them that could match me. For running, fighting, or anything else. Hey, Ingrid? No! Mustn't think of her – that's how all this started. Women! The cause of all trouble. Even the Bible said so, if I remember correctly.

I suppose they are still after me. I haven't actually looked back for a while. No! No looking back. I've outrun them, that's all there is to it. *(Stretches out.)* Aah… whatever – whatever I want to be… *(Dozes off.)*

(CHRYSSIE ENTERS QUIETLY from opposite side of stage. Her clothes are green, and look like they're made from plants. Her hair is untidy, her stockings torn. Her skin is emerald green. One side of her face is tattooed. She sits on a rock in a sunny spot and stretches, equal part slovenly and seductive. SANDY follows, and stands beside her more demurely. Her clothes and skin are pale brown orange, could pass for a deep suntan, with a less intricate tattoo. Neither see PEER.)

CHRYSSIE: Aa-a-a-h… this sunlight isn't so bad really, is it? Certainly not as bad as it's cracked up to be.

. . .

SANDY: It's certainly warming, but in a nice way. I could get to like warmth, I think.

CHRYSSIE: Oh yes, that's nice too. But I was thinking more of the light. I like the way it catches me. Brings out my colour nicely.

SANDY: It certainly does, and it's a good colour.

CHRYSSIE: Of course. It's a royal colour. No offence, Sandy, yours is nice in its own way, too…

SANDY: But it's not quartz. No offence taken. I quite understand. Shall we go on?

CHRYSSIE: I'm in no hurry. It's not like we've anywhere in particular to go, or anything special to do. Resting here, being part of the landscape, is quite enough.

SANDY: As you say. *(Flexes shoulders and legs.)* Still, or not so still, I'd like to move on. Too much sun for too long, and we're likely to get too set. Be stuck here until it's dark.

CHRYSSIE: There are worse fates. As well stuck here as back in the caverns with my family and the others. They're no fun, any of them!

. . .

SANDY: I suppose being the royal family means some level of responsibility.

CHRYSSIE: All show and no fun. It's dull, dull, tedious and dull. Father lives in another world mostly, he's so <u>old</u>. His mother is even worse. His sisters aren't much better. Being taught by them was an endless grind. 'To take my rough edges off,' they'd keep telling me.

SANDY: It never really worked, did it, Chryssie?

CHRYSSIE: No. I <u>like</u> having an edge. Move into the shade if the light worries you, Sandy.

SANDY: *(flexing fingers)* I think I'd better. *(Watching her hands with some concern, she crosses the stage, and almost treads on the sleeping PEER.)* Oh! Chryssie! Chryssie! Look!

CHRYSSIE: What? What's wrong? Oh! Well, look at that. *(She gets up and crosses to stand beside SANDY, both upstage of PEER.)* That's a real flesh-and-blood man, isn't it?

SANDY: I guess so. I've never seen one up close before.

CHRYSSIE: He's quite well put together, isn't he? In a – squishy sort of way.

SANDY: If you like that sort of thing, I suppose.

. . .

CHRYSSIE: Come on, he'd make quite a fetching troll if he hardened up.

SANDY: I can see him fetching you, at least.

CHRYSSIE: Don't be cheeky, Sandy. I <u>am</u> a princess after all. I think he's cute. I wonder if I can keep him?

SANDY: He's human. He'll break.

CHRYSSIE: Well, I won't keep him long, then.

SANDY: No, you never do. *(CHRYSSIE looks up sharply.)* Your playthings, I mean. Oh, alright, have your way. I don't imagine you want or need me around, so I'll go back to the halls.

CHRYSSIE: *(giggles)* If I can't handle a human, there's something very wrong.

SANDY: As long as there isn't anything wrong <u>about</u> handling a human. Oh, don't mind me, Chryssie. If anyone back in the caverns asks, I'll just say you're getting some exercise. It might surprise them, but most know not to ask twice. One telling-off is more than enough.

. . .

(SANDY *exits*. CHRYSSIE *arranges herself interestingly near* PEER, *and starts picking tiny pebbles off the ground – mime – and throwing them at him.* PEER *twitches and waves his hand as if at a fly in his sleep. Eventually one hits a tender spot and he wakes and sits up quickly.*)

PEER: Ow! That was sharp! Nasty insects up here in the hills! *(Looks around, not seeing the green figure near him.)* Huh! Wretched thing must have flown off when I woke up. I even frighten bugs! Wow, I must have been tired. Funny – I thought I heard voices, but there's nobody here. Must have dreamed it. That little snooze seems to have done me a power of good, though. I feel like a new man.

CHRYSSIE: That's funny, so do I.

PEER: Who? Where? What?

CHRYSSIE: Me. Right here. And I'm quite sure you heard me.

PEER: Oh! Er – hello.

CHRYSSIE: *(almost purring)* Hello.

PEER: Yes. Hello. *(Looks more closely at her. Huskily -)* Hello. *(They both stand, looking each other up and down.)* You're... interesting.

CHRYSSIE: Thank you. Yes, I am. And the more you get to know me, the more interesting I become.

. . .

PEER: I'm sure that's true. And, you know, that's also true of me. Oh yes, there's more to me than meets the eye.

CHRYSSIE: Eyes, mmm... *(They gaze into each other's eyes.)*

PEER: It's said that the eyes are the windows to the soul...

CHRYSSIE: Really? Said by who?

PEER: Um, now you mention it... er... no-one important, that I can think of. But it sounds nice. Doesn't it?

CHRYSSIE: I suppose so. I've never thought much about my soul. What do you see through these windows?

PEER: Something – someone, sorry – quite fascinating, I'm sure.

CHRYSSIE: Likewise, I'm sure. Do you see anything that tempts you?

PEER: Ah, yes, and I can resist anything except temptation.

(THEY HOLD HANDS.)

. . .

CHRYSSIE: My name is Chrysoprase.

PEER: That's – unusual. Old family name?

CHRYSSIE: It's a very old family, yes. You can call me Chryssie. Those closest to me do. Would you like to be close to me?

PEER: Stone me, yes!

CHRYSSIE: Stone you? *(She clenches a fist. PEER doesn't notice, but at least senses he's made a mistake.)*

PEER: I'm sorry. A figure of speech.

CHRYSSIE: Not one I've heard. You're not from around here, are you?

PEER: Not too far away, but not here, as such, no. I'm a bit of a wanderer, you see. Making my way in the world. I'm sorry if I offended you, Chryssie – please forgive me!

CHRYSSIE: No offence. Just surprise. But I'm sure I could find a way to forgive you, anyway. *(They embrace, and cuddle willingly for a while.)*

PEER: I can honestly say, I've never met anyone like you before.

. . .

CHRYSSIE: I shouldn't think so. You're unique in my experience, too. Unique and special.

PEER: Special and wonderful. You are, I mean.

CHRYSSIE: Is that really true?

PEER: As true as my name is Peer Tiberius Gynt! As true as that you're a beautiful woman! We could be good together, Chryssie. I'll show you the sort of man I am – imagine never having to work...

CHRYSSIE: I don't.

PEER: Being able to eat all you want, till you can't fit another morsel...

CHRYSSIE: I already do.

PEER: I promise I'll never shout at you, or pull your hair...

CHRYSSIE: And not hit me, either?

PEER: Never! I swear! We sons of kings don't strike our women!

CHRYSSIE: *(double take)* A king's son! Really?

. . .

PEER: Oh, yes.

CHRYSSIE: Well, I'm the daughter of the Mountain King.

PEER: Oh yes? How... suitable!

CHRYSSIE: Further up in the mountains, my father has his own palace.

PEER: Down a ways, my mother has a larger one.

CHRYSSIE: Do you know my father? His name is King Ferrous.

PEER: Do you know my mother? Her name is Queen Victoria.

CHRYSSIE: The mountains themselves reel when my father's angry.

PEER: If my mother starts to go off, the mountains will run for the hills!

CHRYSSIE: Hmmm... Ah, Peer – beside this... interesting outfit, have you any other clothes?

PEER: Of course! You should see my Sunday best! Well, okay, today is Sunday, I know, but...

. . .

CHRYSSIE: I understand. My good 'going-out' clothes are gold and silver.

PEER: And here you are, out, in what look like grasses, leaves and moss. Very attractive grasses, leaves and moss, I must say!

CHRYSSIE: Thank you, kind sir. Peer, there's an important thing you must remember about us – mountain folk. We have an ancient custom that we still take very seriously. Everything we have has a 'double shape'. Things might not be as they first appear to you. So, for example, when you first come to my father's palace, it wouldn't be surprising if at first you thought that it was just a heap of stones and rubbish.

PEER: I get it. It's the same where I come from. You might think our gold and ermine is rust and mildew, or mistake our decorative window panes for rough cardboard or faded cloth.

CHRYSSIE: Black looks like white, and ugly like fair.

PEER: Clean looks like filthy. Big looks small.

CHRYSSIE: Oh, Peer, I can see we're just perfectly suited to each other!

PEER: Like the hair to the comb *(neither has neat hair)* or the foot to the sock – or, er, stockings. Umm... Chryssie, my love, I – umm – can't ask 'your place or mine?', as my palace is – unavailable right now. A wedding. One of the, um, subjects...

. . .

CHRYSSIE: Don't fret, Peer. I know a little spot not far from here, where no-one will disturb us.

PEER: Only the trees and rocks will see us, eh?

CHRYSSIE: Not if they know what's good for them. And afterwards...

PEER: Afterwards?

CHRYSSIE: Afterwards, we can go to my palace.

PEER: *(quietly)* Better yours than mine.

CHRYSSIE: To think, I was feeling so sad and sorry for myself earlier. It just goes to show, you never know what's about to turn up in your life.

PEER: That's certainly true, my dear!

CHRYSSIE: *(whistles)* My steed, my steed! My wedding steed! *(PEER reacts slightly to this)* Come on, brave Hamlet!

PEER: We'll gallop right up to the palace. Afterwards. *(SFX undergrowth crashing, and loud grunting of a large pig approaching.)*

Hamlet, eh? That's a famous name! Great folks are known by the great steeds they ride!

(CHRYSSIE DRAGS OFF PEER.)

BLACKOUT
  (Music fragment: "Next we were moving on, and he was with me, yeah me - I Love Rock and Roll".)

ACT 1, SCENE 3

1:3

(LIGHTS UP.
 Music fragment: "Would you lay with me in a field of stone?"
 PEER lying propped up against a rock or tree, half asleep, twirling a green garter idly, shirt unbuttoned and a dreamy smile on his face.)

PEER: *(to himself)* There's something quite... romantic about this time of day – the sun starting to dip, the long dreamy twilight... *(He sits up, suddenly awake, as CHALKIE enters, apparently hiking.)*

CHALKIE: Peer! Well, I must confess, I'm a little surprised to find you here.

. . .

PEER: Why? It was your idea I go to the mountains.

CHALKIE: That's not quite how I remember it...

PEER: And what a great idea it was! There could be no better place for me!

CHALKIE: Really?

PEER: For one thing, it's not Henriksberg! I'm not exactly welcome there any more, after the fuss at the wedding.

CHALKIE: Well, as you predicted, Ingrid did make her feelings known. She ran away from the ceremony and a few folks had to go after her.

PEER: After <u>her</u>? They were looking for me!

CHALKIE: I don't think... oh, never mind. You're heading for the sea, then?

PEER: That was the plan, but you know, life is what happens while you're making other plans.

CHALKIE: Things have been happening?

. . .

PEER: Oh, yes! I've got high hopes now. Real opportunity to make something of myself.

CHALKIE: Any idea of what?

PEER: *(conspiratorially)* Royalty! Yes, I think that here, my real inner nobility can be recognized and appreciated.

CHALKIE: Inner nobility? Mm – I must admit, Peer, that's not how I'd considered you.

PEER: That's my modest nature, old friend. I've hidden my light under a bushel. You can't blame me – some of the clods I've grown up around.

CHALKIE: Clods, you say?

PEER: Oh yes, thick as bricks, a lot of them.

CHALKIE: There's a lot of that around.

PEER: And so, I learned to hide some of the better parts of my character. I didn't want to embarrass people, or make them too envious, though some obviously always were.

CHALKIE: That's very generous of you.

. . .

PEER: I think so. It avoids confrontation. Not that I'm afraid of a fight! I'll fight any man if I have to!

CHALKIE: I know that. We must talk more about this 'royalty' thing, but first I should ask – how exactly did you come to be... here? My people have places that aren't readily found by... others.

PEER: By humans, you mean? Oh, it's quite alright. I know about the little... differences. I'm not prejudiced. Call me colour blind.

CHALKIE: There is a bit more to it than that.

PEER: Oh, I can be flexible when the situation requires it. As to how I found this place, well, I admit I had some help.

CHALKIE: Help?

PEER: Indeed. While I was wandering – not lost, but let's say aimlessly, I was lucky enough to encounter a beautiful creature, lady, I should say, named Chryssie.

CHALKIE: Chryssie? *(to himself)* There's more than one kind of luck in the world. *(to PEER)* Chrysoprase. The king's daughter.

. . .

PEER: That's how she introduced herself. I must admit it is nice to hear it from an independent source, as it were. You can't always believe everything that people tell you about themselves.

CHALKIE: That's certainly true, Peer.

PEER: We've taken rather a shine to each other.

CHALKIE: Yes, I can imagine Chryssie shining. When it suits her.

PEER: And you know I can be dazzling, when I want to be.

CHALKIE: Mmm.

(CHRYSSIE ENTERS, *rearranging her hair, though it still looks untidy.*)

CHRYSSIE: Oh, hello Sir Chalk. *(PEER reacts with surprise.)*

CHALKIE: *(polite)* Chrysoprase – good to see you.

PEER: *(HALF-JOKINGLY)* NOT 'YOUR MAJESTY'?

CHRYSSIE: We're not in the palace now. *(Snatches back her garter.)*

. . .

CHALKIE: No, we're not. I didn't think you strayed far from the hall.

CHRYSSIE: Oh, I do like going for little walks with Sandy. Does us good to get out. A bit.

PEER: Who's Sandy?

CHRYSSIE: We've been friends forever. She's quite sweet, really.

PEER: She. That's alright.

CHRYSSIE: Why, darling Peer! Are you being jealous?

PEER: Not exactly...

CHALKIE: *(to himself)* Possessive more likely. Royalty, is it? *(to CHRYSSIE)* You've told Peer your – history, I gather?

CHRYSSIE: As much as necessary, er, appropriate, yes. Peer, I want you to meet my father.

PEER: Well, if I'm – we're, to inherit the throne, I'll have to be introduced sooner or later...

CHRYSSIE: Sooner. Definitely sooner!

. . .

PEER: There's no rush, is there? *(Looks back towards his village)* Although, I do prefer to have a roof over my head.

CHALKIE: Can I make a suggestion, Chrysoprase? You know your father's not keen on surprises. It might be wise if you go see him on your own first. Break the news, so his first reaction isn't to break Peer.

CHRYSSIE: He wouldn't dare!

PEER: I should hope not!

CHALKIE: Ferrous is the <u>king</u>, and has been for a very long time. He's set in his ways...

CHRYSSIE: His '<u>WAYS</u>' are rusted on! If he was any more set he'd be immobile.

CHALKIE: True enough. But I know that <u>you</u> can talk him around.

CHRYSSIE: Indeed.

CHALKIE: Keep young Peer out of the danger zone if there's any initial explosion of temper, then you can calm your father down, and introduce our friend in a more peaceful environment.

. . .

Peer: That does sound diplomatic, my dear.

Chryssie: Father <u>can</u> be hard… Alright. I'll go and prepare the king, and the court, for my new consort. Hamlet! Hamlet! Here boy! *(She exits, whistling. Pig noises off as she goes.)*

Peer: 'Sir' Chalk, eh? Where do you fit in the royal scheme of things?

Chalkie: I'm the court… historian.

Peer: Trolls have a long and proud history, I suppose.

Chalkie: Long, anyway. I've also got responsibility for keeping an eye on the outside world. Watch out for anything that's of relevance to us. That's why I can come and go as I please from the king's hall.

Peer: Playing darts is relevant to the troll king?

Chalkie: The pub's the best place to keep up with local news. You know that. Look at that development application for a new road to be put through up here.

Peer: Whatever happened to that?

Chalkie: A few inconvenient rockfalls made the project uneconomical.

. . .

PEER: I see. Convenient coincidence.

CHALKIE: That's right. Of all the gin joints in all the world, Rick's Bar is – well, by Henriksberg standards, a mine of information. Not great for a wider view of things –

PEER: Very true!

CHALKIE: But I read the newspapers, and magazines. Watch the television in the bar. A distorted view of the outside world, much of the time, I admit, but still better than what's available in our caverns. The only view is through the doorway, and there's not many who look out even when it is open.

PEER: All the more reason to think that Chryssie is a bit special, then.

CHALKIE: *(thoughtfully)* I suppose that's true. She and her friend Sandy, both. I wonder who leads who? I know Sandy's naturally a bit curious. She does ask me questions about what I see and hear. So does Chrysoprase, but her questions are different.

PEER: How so?

CHALKIE: She wants things.

. . .

PEER: She is a princess, isn't she?

CHALKIE: Yes. Trolls aren't very ambitious. It's against our nature, especially after infancy. You know, most stones are just rocks that lack ambition.

PEER: What ambition can a rock have?

CHALKIE: To be a troll. That's enough.

PEER: I see. *(He clearly doesn't.)* Who'd have thought? You've been a rock all this time that I've known you.

CHALKIE: A troll, Peer. Calling me, or any troll, a 'rock' is like calling a human an animal. No, some of them do behave that way – more like calling him or her a lump of meat.

PEER: Sorry, mate. I'll try to remember that.

CHALKIE: Wise. I can pass for human, if I'm careful. My colour isn't too unusual amongst you, and I can cover my tattoo with a bit of powder. *(Points to the side of his face.)*

PEER: You are pale, now you mention it. You said you didn't like the sun.

. . .

CHALKIE: And that's true. Of all trolls. If we spend too long in the daylight we get very slow. Eventually, we'll stop moving completely, and start to grow. That happened to my great-uncle Ben, down on the south-east coast of England.

PEER: Ben? Dover?

CHALKIE: Yes. Don't go there. I stay indoors and out of the sunlight as much as possible. I avoid crowds, and close contact, so people don't notice that my 'skin' feels different. Unlike a number of my kin, I can manage a decent conversation. I'm not as dense as others.

PEER: I've always thought you're pretty sharp.

CHALKIE: Good of you to say so. I've worked to knock a lot of my own rough edges off. And I'm careful about what I drink.

PEER: I've never seen you drink anything but vodka, or the odd gin.

CHALKIE: Actually, I'm very fond of good red wine. I never indulge in public. Not human public.

PEER: Why? Does it go to your head?

CHALKIE: Eventually. I did manage a glass at the wedding reception once it all settled down. Before I slipped away. *(Opens shirt to show stomach-shaped red stain.)* Do you remember an old TV commercial for toothpaste – about 'liquid getting into this chalk'?

PEER: A long time ago, yeah… wow…

CHALKIE: Alright, don't stare. It passes.

PEER: I imagine so. *(Curious, he pokes CHALKIE in the stomach. CHALKIE pokes back, gently, but it's enough to double PEER over.)* Ow! Okay, yes, there is a difference! Oh, why am I not stone like thee? Heh, heh – that line rings a bell. Have you ever seen that movie?

CHALKIE: The one about the hunchback? I tried, but I couldn't watch it for long.

PEER: You thought it was that bad?

CHALKIE: Not at all, but I must tell you. Don't make jokes about bells in the caverns. Trolls <u>hate</u> bells.

PEER: Don't find them appealing eh?

CHALKIE: I'm serious. The sound gives us a ringing headache.

PEER: Now who's joking?

. . .

CHALKIE: Not me. *(PEER looks thoughtful, and nods.)* Peer, as a friend – be careful of King Ferrous, if you insist on going to the hall.

PEER: How can I not? There's a throne on offer! And gold, too, I gather.

CHALKIE: There's a gold mine under the hall, yes, but there's not a lot of production. We don't use the stuff for decoration, only trade. You humans like it – for us, it's just another rock, albeit a useful one. And as to that throne, it's just another thing to sit on, and there are lots of those in the world. Be even more careful of Chrysoprase. There are a lot of differences between you two.

PEER: We're kindred spirits, my friend. Our differences are just cosmetic.

CHALKIE: No, they're not. Not between troll and human. Our cultures…

PEER: Culture is like a coat, Chalkie. It can be taken off or put on just as easily, if you've a mind to do it. Look at you!

CHALKIE: All I do is – enough.

BLACKOUT
(Music fragment: "When you really really need it the most, That's When Rock'n'Roll Dreams Come Through".)

ACT 1, SCENE 4

1:4

(IN THE KING'S COURT.
 Music fragment: Greig's "Hall of the Mountain King"
 A well-worn throne on a dais, some scattered rocks or rough chairs. Maybe a tattered wall hanging or two, but mostly grey. Very grey.
 SANDY and CLIFF mid-stage. CLIFF's clothes and skin are grey.
 CITRINE in her chair, playing with an all-grey Rubik's Cube.)

CLIFF: But he's... he's... human!

SANDY: He can't help an accident of birth.

CITRINE: Humans have their place.

In a pot, and on a dish.

CLIFF: She could do so much better than that!

SANDY: Like you, for example?

CLIFF: Why not?

SANDY: Come on, Cliff – she's a princess. You haven't got even a fragment of quartz in your veins.

CLIFF: Maybe not, but I don't have blood in them, either! And I've been a part of this court for years.

(THE SISTERS - ROSE, SMOKIE and AMY enter – pink, brown and purple respectively – and stand near the throne.)

ROSE: Sweeping it, mostly.

CLIFF: No, I don't!

SMOKIE: No, you don't, do you?

CLIFF: I'm the royal guard!

. . .

Amy: Seriously, Cliff, what do you have to guard our brother from?

Sandy: *(quietly)* You three, maybe?

Sisters: Pardon?

Sandy: Sorry – just a cough. Bit of sediment stuck in my throat.

Cliff: I have to protect against Outside or Unwelcome Influences.

Citrine: The outside world is best ignored.
    Such ignorance is its own recompense.

Rose: There isn't much can influence Ferrous if he doesn't want to be.

Smokie: He's rock solid in his determination.

Amy: Except when it comes to his daughter, admittedly.

Rose: Yes, she does have his ear.

Smokie: She's the crab apple of his eye.

Amy: She leads him by the nose.

. . .

SANDY: She does give plenty of cheek.

(THE SISTERS TURN *and stare darkly at her. Clearly, they don't like anyone else intruding on their word-play. SANDY shrugs.*)

CLIFF: Chrysoprase is a princess.

ROSE: So are the three of us.

SMOKIE: Officially.

AMY: You don't see us carrying on as if we're precious. *(Careful silence.)*

ROSE: Young Sandy, what do you know about this – creature that Chrysoprase is bringing home?

SANDY: I've seen him, but that's all.

SMOKIE: What does it look like?

SANDY: Quite well made, I think, as humans go.

AMY: As humans go, they can't go far enough.

. . .

CITRINE: A human once came in here by force -
We served him roasted, with apple gravy.

ROSE: Untrustworthy.

SMOKIE: Unappetizing.

AMY: Unattractive.

ROSE: Sneaky.

SMOKIE: Slimy.

AMY: Squishy.

CLIFF: Scrawny. *(SISTERS glare at him.)* Sorry.

SANDY: But Chryssie must see something in him.

ROSE: She sees something that's different, that's all.

SMOKIE: And something different is all that she ever wants.

. . .

Amy: And whatever Chrysoprase wants –

Sisters: Chrysoprase gets. *(All five trolls sigh.)*

(SFX fanfare – "Rock & Roll Part 1" - KING FERROUS *enters, attended by CHALKIE, and ascends the throne. His staff is a polished stick, his robes faded, his crown perhaps dented and cobwebbed.)*

All *(but King)*: Hail to the King!

King: Yes, hail to me, as is my due.
    My sisters dear, and subjects true,
    Grandmother Citrine, I trust you're well,
    Although, granted, tis often hard to tell.
    I've spoken with my daughter long –
    She's insistent that her feeling's strong.
    A human beau is not the norm
    Yet she's smitten with his form,
    And after due consideration,
    I see value in the situation.

Rose: Value? What? Have you gone soft?
    Bats taken lodging in your loft?

Smokie: You're only asking for division,
    Best reconsider your decision!

King: I shall not! This is my throne -

The decision's mine and mine alone!

AMY: It's Chrysoprase alone you're pleasing,
There can be no other reason.

CLIFF: I hate it when they talk like this.

SANDY: THEY DO IT FOR FERROUS' sake. It makes him more comfortable.

CHALKIE: That, and a certain amount of respect. It was how all trolls spoke, once upon a time. Now even the sisters don't bother much - they just do it when the king is around.

KING: You underestimate my brain, as ever.
My thinking's subtle, and it's clever.
Unlike you, my sisters three,
A longer vision do I see:
New blood is what our line requires
And that tallies with my girl's desires.

CITRINE: Overindulgence is always a danger,
Especially if she consorts with a foreigner.

ROSE: But a human's life is only fleeting!

SMOKIE: In the old days, flesh was just for eating!

AMY: If she should have a halfling child
   It may live longer, but run wild!

KING: Hush! Keep quiet! In calmness bide!
   We can't give in to foolish pride.
   Things have not gone well of late
   We trolls now face a doubtful fate.
   A chance of help that's unexpected
   Must be seen to be respected.
   (PEER enters on CHRYSSIE's arm)
   New blood for the royal line? We'd love it!
   So, lad, 'tis my girl you covet?

PEER: Yes. If she comes complete with kingdom for a dowry.

KING: While I yet live one half is thine,
   After I'm gone, you're next in line.

PEER: I'm content with that.

CLIFF: Huh! Content, he says!

ROSE: Tradition dictates male as heir.

SMOKIE: That's why we've never had our share.

. . .

The Hall of the Mountain King

Amy: Alas, our genders all are wrong,
    Else the throne's where <u>we</u>'d belong.

Citrine: *(licking lips)* You know, I think if I were younger
    There's meat for which I might well grab at.

King: *(to PEER)* But hold, my boy, you must pledge too.
    Break any and your life is through.
    First – you'll live within our halls
    Avoiding where the daylight falls.

Peer: If I'm called 'Your Majesty' here, that won't be hard.

King: Second, see how well you ken
    The difference twixt trolls and men?

Rose: Now we're getting to the truth!

Smokie: Let's see how sharp's his wisdom tooth -
    If he can crack our monarch's quiz.

Amy: A worthy ruler then he is.

King: So, what's the difference you find
    Tween our trolldom and your humankind?

        . . .

PEER: There isn't any, as far as I can gather. Oh, some trolls would fight you, some even eat you – but there are people like that too, given the chance.

KING: Tis true, we're like enough in that,
    But different as sharp to flat
    In how we each our futures view.
    "Man, must to thyself be true,"
    Is proudly said in sunlight's blaze,
    But that my people doth amaze.
    Our philosophy you may think rough:
    "Troll, to thy self be – ENOUGH!"

TROLLS: Enough! Enough! Enough!

CITRINE: *(one extra:)* Enough!

ROSE: Enough is all that we demand.

SMOKIE: The sum and substance of our land.

AMY: So, man, do you understand?

PEER: It, er, seems a little vague. Hazy.

KING: "ENOUGH" – the watchword of this grotto
    Must be your own heartfelt motto.

. . .

PEER: Well… but…

KING: It must be, Peer, you surely see,
   If trolldom's king you wish to be!

PEER: "ENOUGH", eh? It's an – interesting philosophy. Good for a throne, oh, and a lovely girl, of course… hmm… well, if that's how it's got to be, Enough will be enough for me!

BLACKOUT
   (Music fragment: "Call Me King Of The Mountain")

ACT 1, SCENE 5

1:5

(MUSIC FRAGMENT: *"I want to rock'n'roll all night, and party every day."*
The Hall is now empty except for PEER and SANDY, who is hanging some tatty paper decorations – dull faded streamers, etc, around the walls.
PEER watches, not offering to help, but politely getting out of the way when appropriate.)

SANDY: A feast in your honour – bravo, Peer! That's a rare and special thing. Trolls aren't big on honouring anyone, but especially not outsiders.

PEER: Thank you. Um, shouldn't you be getting dressed in your court finery, like everyone else?

. . .

SANDY: As Chryssie's attendant, I'm the most junior member of the court. This is my court finery, I'm afraid. For special occasions we all wear our tails.

PEER: Black tie and tails?

SANDY: No. Just black tails.

PEER: Well, anyway, you look quite fine to me.

SANDY: Flatterer.

PEER: I'm serious. You're an attractive woman. *(Now he tries to assist, but the offer is ignored.)*

SANDY: I'm a troll, Peer. You're not one of us though, are you?

PEER: Ah, but I could be, with time.

SANDY: Then you wouldn't be you.

PEER: But would I be what you wanted?

SANDY: No, you wouldn't. You wouldn't be... real.

. . .

PEER: But if I was to become a troll, I'd be enough.

SANDY: Hmm – I think you'll make a better troll than I am. Perhaps you already are.

PEER: Thank you, I think.

SANDY: You're welcome, if you think that's a good thing.

PEER: Naturally. Oh, I know I'll have to make a few changes.

SANDY: There'll be some... sacrifices expected of you. You'd better have the courage of your convictions, Prince Peer.

PEER: I've got no convictions – I've never been caught. *(Thinks)* Sacrifices. Hmm... *(With transparent casualness, PEER starts to tap on walls and floor.)*

SANDY: What are you doing?

PEER: Just being cautious. Is there an emergency exit?

SANDY: We're trolls. We don't have emergencies.

PEER: *(tapping floor with heel)* Is this bedrock?

. . .

SANDY: No, it's just the floor of this level. There are more caverns below the royal hall. The – earthier trolls live down there. We did have a town called Bedrock, many years ago.

PEER: What happened to it?

SANDY: It passed into legend long ago – troll <u>and</u> human, I believe. Chalkie would know more – it's a page right out of history. Are you serious about an exit?

PEER: Well, er, there might be an emergency I want to emerge from...

(SANDY HANDS PEER A FLAT ROCK, *about the size of his palm.*)

PEER: Looks like a pet rock I had once, when I was a kid. I called it Hudson.

SANDY: I had a little cousin named Hudson. His family lived over in another hill. I suppose it might have been him. What was he like when he grew up?

PEER: Grew up? Umm – I've no idea. I did wonder whatever happened to it – er, him. Lost when we moved house.

SANDY: Well, don't lose this one. You might need it.

. . .

PEER: What for? Luck?

SANDY: Maybe. If you ever do decide to leave this hall, it will work as a key for the big gate at the front. We trolls can just put a couple of fingers in the slot and twist, but all you have are bones. They're not strong enough.

PEER: I'm stronger than I look! (*She grabs his hand and squeezes.*) Ow! Okay – I get your point! Whew – I thought Chryssie played rough...

SANDY: If Chryssie decides to play rough with you, I promise you, you'll go to pieces.

PEER: I'm glad I'm on the right side of her then! I was just, er, being friendly with you, you understand.

SANDY: Oh, I understand. If you actually were a troll, I think you'd be something like mica. You're pretty transparent. *(Quietly)* And disappointingly shallow. *(Exit.)*

(CLIFF CARRIES ON A SMALL TABLE, *covered with a garish tablecloth, and places it in front of the throne. PEER, behind him, directs the table be moved slightly. CLIFF complies, but growls.*)

PEER: You don't like me much, do you, Cliff?

. . .

CLIFF: Not true. I don't like you at all.

PEER: But why? I've done you no harm. We could even get to be friends, with time. Maybe. Perhaps.

CLIFF: You're weak. Soft. Fleshy. Thin-skinned. Breakable.

PEER: Of course, by your standards, yes. I am human...

CLIFF: Exactly. You don't belong here.

PEER: That's not your decision to make, though, is it? The king himself has made me welcome. This party was his idea. And his daughter, dear Chryssie, has opened her heart to me.

CLIFF: Not all she opened.

PEER: Don't be vulgar. That's your princess you're talking about.

CLIFF: Yeah, mine. Not yours.

(CHALKIE ENTERS, now wearing an all-white jester's hat and patched clown costume. At least one button is a big ball of cotton wool.)

. . .

CHALKIE: Well, Peer, you've got it made, my friend. A banquet in your honour. It seems you're winning Ferrous over about as well as you've won Chryssie.

PEER: Chalkie? That's an... unusual outfit you're wearing.

CLIFF: Sir Chalk is the official Court Fool.

PEER: Fool? As in, jester? I thought you were the court historian.

CHALKIE: All history is a joke, but none more so than ours. But this is an auspicious occasion. It's been a long time since this court welcomed new blood.

CLIFF: *(sneers)* Blood – huh! From the land of light.

CHALKIE: There are still some who'd rather dwell in darkness.

("Rock and Roll Part 1" *fanfare, and the KING enters, followed by his SISTERS, and CITRINE. All have added 'formal wear' to their costumes - a cloak and a black tail with a coloured bow.*)

KING: Welcome all, to this event
    Quite without recent precedent.
    To a foreigner of princely station
    We dedicate this grand occasion.
    Bring forth our finest cakes and mead. (*AMY and SMOKIE exit.*)

What greater pleasure than to feed?

PEER: Well, certainly I'm honoured, Your Highness. And looking forward to sharing in your magnificence.

CHALKIE: Have a care, Peer. Manage your expectations.

PEER: Oh, you know me - I expect nothing.

CLIFF: That's more than you deserve.

CHALKIE: You won't be disappointed, then.

KING: Prince Peer, I bid you sit, at least -
You're guest of honour at this feast.
Simple and humble we like our fare
And you must learn our tastes to share.
(AMY and SMOKIE enter with a platter of food, which looks like cowpats, and a flagon and goblet – either or both of which are clear, containing a liquid that's the colour of old urine. SMOKIE and AMY exit again.)
Our cows give cakes, our oxen wine
With time, you'll find their taste divine.
If your first impression's something crude
Remember they're home-baked, home-brewed,
So, if neither is quite to your taste,
Just remember, we're avoiding waste!

. . .

PEER: *(pushing the things away)* That smells like – never mind! And that home brew is surely made from -

CITRINE: The mead's origin is not a riddle.
   It's made from finest hill-cow's water.

KING: To him who takes the golden brew,
   Shall go my girl, and royal throne, too.

PEER: Of course, we're told that a man shouldn't trust first impressions. I suppose, at least, it's all organic. I could get used to the taste, and smell, with time. Lots of time. *(sips)*

KING: Now you're showing clearer wit.
   But hold – did I just see you spit?

PEER: Sorry, force of habit. I was, er, trained in wine tasting in my younger days in the royal court.

(AMY ENTERS WITH ROUGH CLOTHES.)

KING: Now your outworld clothes you'll doff.
   Their fashion here is frankly off.
   (PEER sheds his clothes and puts on troll-wear handed to him by AMY, coarser but in the same colours. He surreptitiously transfers his phone and the flat rock when SANDY reminds him, before she exits.)
   All we wear is mountain-made –
   Our fabrics, furs and fine brocade.

The only thing from valley sales
Is the silk we tie about our tails.

PEER: I don't have a tail!

KING: Then we shall find one you can don.
    (to ROSE) My Sunday best tail – fix it on!

ROSE: Your best adornment? On this... creature?
    If you insist, but it's a wasted feature.
    Tails were once our pride and joy.
    It shouldn't be a human's toy!

(ROSE RUMMAGES in a chest at the back of stage.)

AMY: There was a time in our race's days long gone
    When every troll had a tail of their own,
    In only a handful of generations
    We lost that pride, in fast mutations.
    A loss we still with grief lament
    And wonder where our spine-ends went
    The silks are all by which we recollect
    What we think helped us first stand erect.

CITRINE: A troll's tail once was pride and glory.
    A symbol of our race's story.
    My grandfather's tail, when I was young –
    I remember it. He was well-endowed.

        . . .

(ROSE, over next few lines ties a tail around PEER.)

PEER: No, you don't! I'll look ridiculous!

CITRINE: To give a human trollish class
    Takes more than a tail tied to his backside!

KING: If Chrissie's heart, and throne, you'd trump
    It won't be with a tail-less rump!

PEER: Making a beast of a man!

KING: No, no, my son. You misconstrue.
    It's thus you will more courtly woo.
    And as a mark of highest honour
    Your bow shall be of bright flame colour.

PEER: We're taught, of course, to respect the conventions, even unconventional conventions, of those with ways different to our own. So be it. Tie away. *(PEER wags tail and struts around.)*

KING: Now at last, good sense you see.
    Ere long you'll find you're just like me.

ROSE: See how nicely it can wag and wave.
    You make quite a handsome rogue-ish knave.

        . . .

PEER: What next? Do you expect me to give up my family's Christian faith?

KING: No, faith is something you may keep
    Be it shallow, be it deep.
    What's within is not important,
    What matters is a troll's deportment.
    Just <u>look</u> like us and there'll be no errors,
    Though your heart's beliefs might give us terrors

PEER: In spite of your many conditions, you're actually quite reasonable.

KING: Trolls oft are better than our reputations,
    Another difference twixt our stations.

(SANDY ENTERS, bows and approaches the KING.)

SANDY: Your daughter and sister have told me to advise the court that the entertainment is ready.

PEER: Oh, excellent!

CHALKIE: Oh, dear.

KING: Tis time our serious business ceased
    Let merriment now be released!

My family's talents, pure and bright
Our eyes and ears shall soon delight.
Let fingers dance across the strings
While fair feet dance on other things.

(SMOKIE AND CHRYSSIE ENTER. SMOKIE plays a guitar or ukulele badly, while CHRYSSIE, veiled, does a clumsy version of a harem dance.)

KING: Such talent ever gives me joy!
    Tell me what do you think, my boy?

PEER: Think of it? Well, ah –

KING: Come, come, good Prince – you may speak free.
    Tell me what you hear and see.

PEER: See? A cow banging her hoof on an untuned string, and a sow pretending to dance to it.

CHALKIE: Oh Peer, you idiot…

ROSE: Eat the wretch! Insulting lizard!

SMOKIE: A cow indeed! I'll roast his gizzard!

KING: Remember before you take offences:

He sees and hears with human senses.

AMY: If that is how he sees and hears
　　　Then tear out his eyes and cut off his ears!

CLIFF: Let me! I'll do it!

CHRYSSIE: *(upset)* Is that any way to talk to Aunt Smokie and I, when we've been entertaining you?

PEER: Oh! Was that you? Sorry! We all make jokes at parties – no offence intended!

CHRYSSIE: Will you swear to me you were only joking?

PEER: Oh, absolutely! The music and dancing were delightful.

KING: This human nature's quite a thing.
　　　Persistently we see it cling.
　　　Hard and strong it may be fought,
　　　But any scars soon fade to naught. *(Pause)*

CITRINE: Those things that make a man a man
　　　Are served best fried in a cast iron pot!

KING: I'm pondering my son-in-law

Who's human – could be, would be, more.
He now <u>seems</u> accommodating:
"I'll do this or that," he's fond of stating.
Our clothes he'll wear most willingly.
Our music, hearken thrillingly.
Mead he'll drink, with some – slight – relish,
And a tail his rump doth now embellish.
But yet I fear that in the finish
That convert's will may well diminish.
To truly see a troll's world view
Some surgery we'll have to do. *(ROSE rushes out)*
A treatment to ensure remission
Of this sad human condition.

PEER: Er – what do you propose to do?

KING: A scratch across your left-hand eye
    And your faulty vision goes awry.
    A deeper gouge upon your right -
    That will balance up your sight.
    For you to see as troll-king should
    Thy windows must be fixed for good...

PEER: You're mad!

(ROSE ENTERS with a tray of sharp implements)

KING: My sister Amy, clever maid
    Has talent at the glazier's trade.
    You'll soon perceive your bride's true beauty

Not sows and cows on music duty.
Cliff – stop him from taking flight
Whilst Amy rightens up his sight.

(CLIFF LUMBERS forward to grasp PEER's arms)

CHALKIE: I knew this wouldn't end well!

PEER: This is madness!

CLIFF: IT'S KING FERROUS' word. He's the wise one – it's you that's mad.

KING: Come, come, my boy – you'll change your story
　　Once you see your bride's true glory.
　　Your troubles be alleviated,
　　Worries, too, abbreviated.
　　Think on this, too, to calm your fears:
　　The eye's the source of bitter tears.

PEER: Well, that is true, and it does say in the old family Bible: "If thine eye offend thee, pluck it out." *(CLIFF releases him, and at a nod from the KING stands back.)* And at some point, my sight <u>will</u> recover, and I'll go back to seeing as I do now...

KING: No, it won't my dear young friend.
　　You'll see thus till your final end.

· · ·

Peer: What?!? Then I'm afraid I must decline, with thanks!

King: Your words, they leave me rather vexed.
    What might you reckon to do next?

Peer: To leave here!

Cliff: Hah! Skinny chance of that!

Rose: But soft! Such thought you must amend.
    Troll laws may break, but never bend.

Smokie: You'll live and die here, foolish mortal –
    This hall has just a one-way portal.

Amy: You talked your way within, no doubt,
    But the troll king's gates don't open out!

Peer: You surely don't mean to detain me by force?

Citrine: The use of force is hardly needy
    To hold a human, weak and scrawny.

King: Young would-be Prince, heed reason's call.
    You're quite cut out to be a troll.
    You bear yourself in our tradition,

And to rule here still is your ambition?

PEER: Of course. In return for a bride and a well-founded kingdom I'm not unwilling to sacrifice something; but all things have their natural limit. I've taken a tail, that's true, but I can always undo the knots and get rid of it. I've shed my old clothes, but they're patched and past their best – possibly quite suitable here, in fact, but I could certainly put them back on if I'd a mind to. *(to himself)* Surely, I'll find it not so hard to adapt to this Trollish way of life. I can easily swear that a cow is a woman, my aunt-in-law even, because an oath's quite an easy thing to break, I've found. But to know that I'll never be free to leave, or ever live as I did... to make that... commitment...*(to KING)* Not even to die as a man, but end my days as a mountain troll, to never leave or pass out those gates as your sisters said, not even in death – that's something I can't submit to!

KING: Now, for my sins, I'm getting annoyed!
   This responsibility that you'd avoid
   Is not a light or casual thing.
   Remember Peer – I am the king!
   You've had your way with...

PEER: Ooh, that's a lie!

KING: ...with my green delight,
   Now you'll marry her to make things right!

PEER: Do you dare accuse me of ---?

. . .

KING: Can you now stand and flat deny her -
　　Who was object of your whole desire?

PEER: Not my <u>whole</u> desire. I admit, the throne's pretty attractive. But yes, I'll admit, I wanted Chryssie, just like she wanted me – isn't that right?

CHRYSSIE: Well, yes… at the time… I suppose…

PEER: But it was no more than that! So, what the devil does <u>that</u> matter?

KING: By Trollish law, the matter's this:
　　A child makes needful wedded bliss.
　　For both of you to think of mating
　　Is just as good as conjugating.

ROSE: The <u>mind</u> is parenting's true source
　　Far better than that 'intercourse'!

SMOKIE: You humans prattle of your soul
　　But your wants, in truth, do make you whole.

AMY: For trolldom it is such desires
　　Alone that light parental fires.

PEER: This is nonsense! I don't – I won't believe any of these lies!

. . .

CHRYSSIE: They're not lies! I wish they were.

KING: It matters not what else you'd rather!
    Ere the year is out you'll be a father!

PEER: Unlock the doors, I'm going.

KING: The brat you'll get in she-goat's skin
    To raise it with your fleshly kin.

PEER: I wish I could wake up!

KING: We'll send it to your palace door,
    And ever after do no more.

PEER: Oh, send it to the Parish orphanage!

KING: Just as you wish, that's your affair.
    It matters not what's done out there.
    Whate'er you choose, you can be sure
    Your legacy will long endure.
    One cannot now undo the past
    And such a mongrel will grow fast.

. . .

PEER: Oh, come, old chap, don't come at me like an avalanche! Fair maiden, be reasonable! Let's come to terms. If there is to be a child, it really should stay here with you.

SANDY: He's making it worse for himself.

CHALKIE: If he digs a much bigger hole, he'll be down in the mines.

PEER: I have to confess that I'm neither a prince, nor rich. Sorry! Whatever way you look at it, you haven't made much of a bargain, I'm afraid.

CHRYSSIE: Your princedom wasn't all you offered me! There was – more.

PEER: I didn't want to be wanted just for my body! I'd like to be wanted for my mind!

CHALKIE: You'd better make one up, then.

PEER: I have! I've made up my mind to get out of here!

CLIFF: What about the princess?

PEER: She's all yours.

. . .

CLIFF: After *you've* had her?

PEER: I never 'had' her.

KING: We do despise
    Your rancid lies!

CITRINE: I had one once, a long time back.
    I think it broke – I remember the 'snap'.

PEER: I mean it! Really. She needed... needs... someone hard as a rock. And that's not me. I'm only human.

SANDY: Really?

PEER: Yes! Ok, I admit, the spirit was willing, but the flesh was weak. Well, not hard enough.

ROSE: Your spirit, it was willing, though?

PEER: Yeah, sure, I'll admit that.

SMOKIE: For us, that is what matters so!

AMY: All trolls from their youth do know

Tis intentions make the birthing grow.

PEER: Definitely a nightmare! Damned for a thought!

KING: I've had enough of lies and moans!
    Dash his brains out on the stones!

SANDY: *(steps in CLIFF's way as PEER grabs CHALKIE's arm.)* Please don't! It's me that'll have to clean up the mess!

CHRYSSIE: Get out of the way!

SANDY: But humans have so much blood in them.

CLIFF: Yes, they do! *(Between them, she and CHALKIE manage to edge CLIFF into upsetting the tray of tools, adding to the chaos.)*

PEER: What can I do now?!?

CHALKIE: Have you kept some charge in your phone, as I advised?

PEER: It's not like I could use it in here. I'm sure there's some life left in the battery.

. . .

The Hall of the Mountain King

CHALKIE: Then there's some life left in Peer Gynt. Play your ring tone – as loud as possible.

PEER: What?

CHALKIE: Your <u>ring</u> tone!

PEER: Ah – yes! *(pulls phone from pocket and frantically punches buttons.)*

(SFX OLD-FASHIONED PHONE RINGING. *CHALKIE pulls a cotton ball button off his costume and plugs his ears, handing some to SANDY. All TROLLS but those two and CITRINE fall about clutching their ears.)*

KING: From whence now comes this awful chime?
    Who dares commit this heinous crime?

CLIFF: *(from the floor)* Him! Your would-be son-in-law!

CITRINE: What's the matter with all of you?
    Why all this fuss and mad to-and-fro?

(SANDY NUDGES *CHALKIE* TO *remind him to fall about clutching ears, like the others)*

PEER: And now they've seen the last of me!
    A good thing that I've got a key. *(Pulls flat rock from pocket)*

Hell's bells – now they've got me doing it! *(Exits at a run.)*

KING: Someone our honour must defend!
    Get after him and apprehend!

CHALKIE: Sorry sire, I can't hear you over the bells.

SANDY: Neither can I.

CITRINE: Useless guard – he dashed right past –
    It's been too long since I moved that quickly.

KING: First wedding, now capture both capsized.
    I cannot move! I'm paralysed!

ROSE: The scoundrel now is taking flight
    Fearful of thy regal might.

SMOKIE: Our gate shall never let him out!

AMY: Don't be too sure, he's a cunning lout.

CHRYSSIE: *(kicking CLIFF)* Go get him! Don't let him get away!

CLIFF: What? You want him back?

. . .

CHALKIE: After the trouble he's made, why want him back?

SISTERS: Vengeance!

CITRINE: Food!

ROSE: The villain's taken to his heels
    And with him go the frightful peals -
    I think my head is slightly clearing
    Slowly I regain my hearing...

SMOKIE: My senses still are overwrought
    Can't see, nor hear, scarce make a thought

AMY: Someone must go after him
    It can't be me – my head's a-swim!

CHRYSSIE: You're supposed to be the royal guard – get up and get him, dead or alive!

CLIFF: Do I get to choose?

KING: After that, his welcome's through.
    If he comes back, his life is, too.

. . .

(CLIFF STRUGGLES *to his feet and lurches off.*)

CHALKIE: Do you think he's managed to get out?

SANDY: He should – I gave him a gate key.

CHALKIE: Well done.

SANDY: I hope when he gets out, he keeps going.

CHALKIE: He will, if I know Peer Gynt. One thing you can rely on about him, when the going gets tough,

SANDY: That's when he gets going? He'd better, for his sake.

CHALKIE: And ours. At least we know he can outrun Cliff.

SANDY: So could a lava flow.

CHRYSSIE: He might be all the evil things you say, and I can't argue with any of that - but he's left me with child! What am I supposed to do now?

ROSE: Lout and villain as a sire?

. . .

SMOKIE: Even you should more aspire!

AMY: You're the daughter of a king
   Why would you do such a thing?

KING: He'll be father yes, but ruler never
   All ties with humankind you'll sever.
   Give him not another thought.
   Your child shall be raised here, at court.
   Though its sire be made of other stuff
   It shall live as troll, and be enough.

BLACKOUT
   (Music: Greig's "Hall of the Mountain King".)

CURTAIN

(above and below) Cast of the May 2025 Lismore Theatre Company production

(Top L-R) Shae Salmon - Rose; Lola Crawley - Smokie; Jenny Craig - Amy; Morgan Montague-Elliott - Cliff; Audrey O'Donnell-Parr - Sandy; Graham Andrews - Chalkie; Brian Fry - Ferrous; Sylvia Clarke - Citrine

(Below) Maitraya Stewart - Peer; Jenni Law - Chrysoprase

Authentic runes used as facial markings and set decoration in the May 2025 Lismore Theatre Company production.

ACT 2, SCENE 1

2:1

(MUSIC: NERO & THE GLADIATORS' "Hall of the Mountain King". Fades down.)

(Lights up: Rick's bar.
CHALKIE stands, sipping a vodka and looking bemusedly at a colourful poster.
Music fragment: "Rock And Roll Music" plays briefly as he reads and fades down.)

CHALKIE: "Iggy Coaldust and the Rock Spiders from Bars. Live at the Upper Cavern". Not quite original, but interesting, I suppose. I wonder how the big debut gig is going?

. . .

(As CHALKIE DRINKS, BOULDER enters, looking equal parts downcast and defiant. He looks like his father PEER, but his hair and one half of his face are green. No tattoos.)

CHALKIE: Hello, lad. I didn't expect you to be here. What's happened to the concert?

BOULDER: It's still going. Just not with me.

CHALKIE: The Rock Spiders decided that they don't need you?

BOULDER: I don't need them.

CHALKIE: Ah. I believe the term is 'musical differences'?

BOULDER: Huh, yeah. I have talent, and they don't.

CHALKIE: They're still playing, though? I take it that the crowd didn't quite see things your way.

BOULDER: What can you expect? Ignorant humans. Eardrums so soft they can't handle real rock.

CHALKIE: Mm. They're not equipped to appreciate a real gravel voice. *(Waves poster.)* Er, I have to ask – 'Iggy Coaldust'?

. . .

BOULDER: Short for Igneous. Much better than what I was stuck with originally. I mean, do I look like a "Chip"?

CHALKIE: Not much, admittedly, although you do bear a striking resemblance to the old block, Peer.

BOULDER: Don't mention that name in my presence!

CHALKIE: Fair enough, fair enough. But Ch… er, lad, you're not igneous either. The quartz on the troll side of your family is all sedimentary.

BOULDER: Uh. Alright. I'm destined for the throne eventually – I want a name that's got some strength about it. Something weighty. I know! Boulder! Yes – that'll do me. *(CHALKIE shrugs.)* Boulder. That's the name I'm taking back to the palace with me.

CHALKIE: You've had enough of the human world, then?

BOULDER: I've never fitted in.

CHALKIE: Well, one half of your heritage is a little hard to hide.

BOULDER: Oh, that hasn't been a problem. I'm a rock singer. We're expected to look different.

. . .

CHALKIE: You're a singing rock, not quite the same thing. On the subject of looking, did you ever catch up with P– , with your father?

BOULDER: He'd be in trouble if I did! But I'm not looking for him – I've <u>never</u> looked for him. I just wanted to… explore a bit.

CHALKIE: What did you find?

BOULDER: Nothing worth pursuing.

CHALKIE: Hmm, not like your father, then. You've spent plenty of time in the daylight. Look at how quickly you've grown in ten years.

BOULDER: That's not my fault.

CHALKIE: *(to himself)* Growing bigger isn't the same as growing up. I didn't say it was a fault. Cross-breeding can be unpredictable. There aren't a lot of hybrids recorded in troll history. There's not a lot of anything recorded in troll history, to be honest. There have been half-breeds over many years, but they mostly seem to have stayed out in the human world.

BOULDER: Doing what?

CHALKIE: It's hard to know. Bare-knuckle fighting? Circus attractions? Politics?

. . .

BOULDER: Huh, none of that for me. I'm going back to the mountains. Back to the hall.

CHALKIE: *(after a pause)* Are you finding that the sun is slowing you down?

BOULDER: No! I can avoid it, anyway. I love the nightlife.

CHALKIE: In Henriksberg? There's not much of it here.

BOULDER: Hah! I can create life wherever I go!

CHALKIE: I have heard rumours. I thought you'd found nothing worth pursuing?

BOULDER: <u>They</u> pursued <u>me</u>!

CHALKIE: Of course.

BOULDER: But I've had enough of that. I've outgrown all that.

CHALKIE: All that? Or all those 'new lives'? Responsibility isn't something you can just grow out of.

. . .

BOULDER: What can't be outgrown, I'll simply disown. *(Both do a double take at the rhyme.)*

CHALKIE: It's been a while. What sort of a welcome do you think you might get at the palace?

BOULDER: I can always talk my way in to anywhere. And if I can't I'll force my way in.

CHALKIE: There's both sides of your heritage, right there.

BOULDER: The best of both worlds, you mean.

CHALKIE: Not quite what I said. All I'm suggesting is –

BOULDER: Don't you worry about me. Me, I'm more than enough! *(Strides off.)*

CHALKIE: What of, I wonder?

BLACKOUT
(Music: "I'm A Rocker, I'm a roller, I'm a right out of controller".)

ACT 2, SCENE 2

2:2

(*LIGHTS UP: the Hall.*
　Music fragment: "Cobblestone mountain, it was made by hand, from the magic and the mortar in a cobblestone land."
　CHRYSSIE is walking angrily, with CLIFF a half-pace behind.)

CLIFF: I tell you, he just rolled in through the front gate, and demanded to see the king!

CHRYSSIE: And you let him?

CLIFF: What could I do? He's the royal grandson. <u>Your</u> son and heir.

. . .

CHRYSSIE: Not if I have anything to say about it. The 'heir' bit at least. That's going to be my throne!

CLIFF: Not according to troll tradition. Only males...

CHRYSSIE: Don't you start that again. I know that's your only interest in me.

CLIFF: That's not true. You're important to me, as you, not as Princess Chrysoprase.

CHRYSSIE: If you say so. And from now on, that will be Princess Jade. It sounds more regal.

CLIFF: Um, okay.

CHRYSSIE: How did my father react?

CLIFF: You know how he is about family.

CHRYSSIE: Of course. Welcomed him with open arms, gave him the run of the place immediately...

CLIFF: Yes, pretty much like you've got. Last I heard, the boy had gone down to the mines.

. . .

CHRYSSIE: What does he want there?

CLIFF: A 'TOUR OF INSPECTION', Boulder apparently said.

CHRYSSIE: Who is Boulder?

CLIFF: That's what he's calling himself now.

CHRYSSIE: Why? What's wrong with Chip?

CLIFF: Maybe he doesn't reckon it's regal enough.

CHRYSSIE: Don't be smart.

CLIFF: Me? Never.

(BOULDER ENTERS. He and CLIFF face off for a moment, before CHRYSSIE pats CLIFF's arm and sends him off. She then sits in front of the throne.)

BOULDER: Mother.

CHRYSSIE: Son. It's been... quite some time.

. . .

BOULDER: I was busy.

CHRYSSIE: That's... good.

BOULDER: Some of it, yeah. Not all.

CHRYSSIE: Did you – er – catch up with your father?

BOULDER: No! Why would I? I don't want anything to do with him, whatever your ideas on the subject might be.

CHRYSSIE: What's that supposed to mean?

BOULDER: You went looking for him when I was still a kid! You tried to give me back to him!

CHRYSSIE: No! I wouldn't let you go. All I wanted was to torment him. With your presence. With <u>our</u> presence. He thought he'd found happiness, love even, with this girl Solveig. No chance! Every day I'll be here watching you and her, I said. Every day. And of course, I demanded he look after you.

BOULDER: I remember that – all too well.

CHRYSSIE: To do his share, I meant. Not to abandon you to him – I'd have been with you day and night, haunting him and his woman.

And again, into the night he fled.

BOULDER: This time you didn't pursue him.

CHRYSSIE: It was your grandfather's insistence that you be brought back and raised at court, as a worthy heir.

BOULDER: By Sir Chalk, and all too often, by the king's wretched sisters. That was tough to endure.

CHRYSSIE: And in the end, you didn't. You took after your father, and ran away.

BOULDER: I took responsibility for my own education. I went out, and I learned.

CHRYSSIE: Learned what?

BOULDER: The ways of the outside world. In time, I knew I'd learned enough.

CHRYSSIE: Oh yes? What did it teach you?

BOULDER: That it's no place for me. This is where I really belong.

. . .

CHRYSSIE: What do you propose to do here?

BOULDER: You're the one that called me a worthy heir.

CHRYSSIE: That's a long way off.

BOULDER: Time will tell, mother. Time will tell. *(Exits.)*

CHRYSSIE: <u>I</u> produced <u>that</u>! What was I thinking? I wasn't, was I? Not with my brain, anyway. Of course, I wasn't the only one – it's not all my fault.

CHALKIE: *(Entering, says quietly)* Nothing ever is. Greetings, Chrysoprase.

CHRYSSIE: Jade. Henceforth, I shall be Princess Jade.

CHALKIE: Really? Okay – as you wish. You seem… disturbed, Jade.

CHRYSSIE: Did you know that Chip has come back?

CHALKIE: Yes. Boulder, he calls himself now.

. . .

CHRYSSIE: I gather so. There's nothing wrong with the name he was given. He's barged into the hall, my father's kowtowing to him already – the brat's got his eye on the throne, you know.

CHALKIE: I didn't, but I'm not surprised. He's inherited ambition.

CHRYSSIE: Ambition is fine. But not ahead of me. He's got to know his place.

CHALKIE: He's a halfling, though. That might count against him, eventually, depending on any available alternatives. No offspring for you and Cliff?

CHRYSSIE: After <u>that</u> experience? No. Not something either of us want.

CHALKIE: And for trolls, it's desire that's the true father of a child. Much better than that messy, hit-or-miss method of human reproduction.

CHRYSSIE: Which I've never understood. Or wanted to.

CHALKIE: They have this thing called a 'maternal instinct'.

CHRYSSIE: Sounds awful. We trolls have better instincts.

. . .

CHALKIE: A strong instinct for self-interest, certainly. But so do most humans.

CHRYSSIE: I wonder... could my son be distracted from his ambitions?

CHALKIE: Find him a hobby? He's a bit old for that, surely. He did pursue a music career, but it got away from him.

CHRYSSIE: Take your Fool's hat off. Not a hobby – a more comprehensive distraction. A family.

CHALKIE: I think that's a road he's travelled, out there, briefly. No enthusiasm for it, he indicated.

CHRYSSIE: Oh, I don't mean with some insubstantial human creature. Too frail and transient. But if I arranged something with a troll female – solid, a dependable anchor.

CHALKIE: Dependable for who?

CHRYSSIE: Me, of course. Someone under orders to keep... Boulder, occupied.

CHALKIE: You've got somebody in mind, don't you?

CHRYSSIE: Of course. Sandy.

. . .

CHALKIE: What do you think her opinion of your idea will be?

CHRYSSIE: Her opinion? She'll do as she's instructed. She <u>is</u> my attendant, and has been for a long time.

CHALKIE: She's been your friend for even longer.

CHRYSSIE: Times change. My needs have changed.

CHALKIE: I think that a lot has changed.

CHRYSSIE: It hasn't changed enough.

BLACKOUT
 (Music fragment: "I'm Not Your Stepping Stone".)

ACT 2, SCENE 3

2:3

(LIGHTS UP ON THE HALL.
  Music fragment: "We will, we will, rock you!"
  CHRYSSIE is sizing up the throne.
  CLIFF is measuring with a piece of rope, comparing the throne's width and height off the ground with her girth and leg length.)
  (BOULDER enters and watches, unnoticed, for a few moments.)

BOULDER: I think it'll fit you well, Mother.

CHRYSSIE: Oh! What? What are you doing here?

BOULDER: Watching.

. . .

CLIFF: You do a lot of that.

BOULDER: It's how I learn.

CLIFF: I watch a lot, too.

CHRYSSIE: You don't learn so much, though, do you? *(Pats CLIFF's arm condescendingly.)*

BOULDER: There's no reason it can't be yours, you know.

CHRYSSIE: What can't?

BOULDER: That throne.

CLIFF: It's supposed to be for males...

BOULDER: Is that a law, or just something that everyone's gotten used to?

CHRYSSIE: Trolls don't have a lot of laws.

CLIFF: Too hard to remember anything complicated.

. . .

CHRYSSIE: For many, yes. But we do know what's right and wrong.

BOULDER: Right and wrong for ourselves, yes.

CHRYSSIE: There's a long tradition to be overcome.

BOULDER: If you were a slave to tradition, I wouldn't have been born, would I?

CLIFF: That's true.

BOULDER: Surely, it's just a matter of your strength of will, isn't it? Your determination?

CHRYSSIE: Ye-e-es... What are you up to? Why so... supportive?

BOULDER: You're my mother. Of course I'm going to support you.

CLIFF: Well, he is part human, I suppose.

BOULDER: There is a degree of self-interest, I admit. With you as queen, I'd be one step closer to the throne myself. As next in line, I mean.

. . .

CHRYSSIE: A very long time off.

BOULDER: Naturally. I'd expect no less.

CHRYSSIE: Mm. But that does raise one other, obvious, small impediment. Ferrous.

CLIFF: He's not small.

BOULDER: No, but he's not young, either. Or well.

CLIFF: Eh?

BOULDER: Haven't you noticed? Maybe it's because I've been – away – for a while, but he seems much slower than I remember. And not just physically. He doesn't have the same grip on things that he used to have. I think he's losing control.

CLIFF: Of what?

BOULDER: The kingdom. The court. Himself. I'm not even sure he really <u>wants</u> to rule any longer.

CHRYSSIE: Really?

. . .

BOULDER: It's a thought. There could be a space there for you to step right into, with some gentle nudging.

CLIFF: Gentle...

BOULDER: It's been well known for a long time that your father hates refusing you anything.

CHRYSSIE: The throne is a different matter.

BOULDER: Why? He's not doing anything with it. Not like you would. If he can be convinced that he'd be comfortable, and well looked after...

CHRYSSIE: There's another problem. Three of them. Rose, Smoke and Amethyst. My three aunts. Even if Ferrous could be convinced to abdicate in favour of a female, they'd fight tooth and nail to change his mind. Or else insist that one of them take over in his place.

BOULDER: Which one? The biggest, the strongest, or the smartest?

CLIFF: Hard to say. The three of them are usually of one mind on most things.

CHRYSSIE: Publicly, at least. If they do argue, they keep it to themselves.

. . .

BOULDER: They couldn't be turned against each other?

CHRYSSIE: It's hard to imagine. They defend themselves and each other with the same ferocity. Even more than they defend their brother.

BOULDER: In return, he defends them. Right?

CHRYSSIE: Of course. Well, it's not so obvious. He doesn't have to. Nobody much criticizes them.

CLIFF: Nobody would dare.

CHRYSSIE: That's part of it. Also, they don't <u>do</u> very much to upset anyone. Except when they were trying to teach you. Although Ferrous usually took your side.

CLIFF: Same as when you were younger. They don't want very much, either. They order people about sometimes, but it's for show. They just want to be comfortable, and left alone.

BOULDER: Why are they here? Beyond the now irrelevant teaching duties, what function do they have?

CLIFF: Function isn't important for trolls.

. . .

BOULDER: You're a guard, aren't you? And there are miners, attendants, the Fool – what you're saying is: function isn't important for <u>royal</u> trolls.

CHRYSSIE: I understand. Being royal is function enough.

BOULDER: It is, if you do enough with it. And the three of them are wasting it. All they're really doing is getting in your way.

CLIFF: I don't think...

CHRYSSIE: No, you don't. That's not your function.

BOULDER: But you do.

CHRYSSIE: That's right. And right now, I think that my three aunts should be convinced that their presence here is no longer desirable.

BOULDER: Well, it's not desirable for you. The trick is for it not be desirable for them. Do you have any ideas?

CHRYSSIE: I always have ideas. Are you willing to help?

BOULDER: Willing, of course, but I doubt I can be effective. I'll talk to Ferrous. There's no chance of his sisters paying attention to anything I say.

. . .

CLIFF: They won't ever listen to me, either.

CHRYSSIE: It isn't a problem. I understand what motivates them. And what will – move them. I can do enough.

BLACKOUT
   (Music fragment: "And where do we go from here? Rock on!".)

ACT 2, SCENE 4

2:4

(Lights up on the Hall.
   Music fragment: "Been a long time, been a long time..."
   The SISTERS are centre stage, CHRYSSIE is near the throne, sitting on the arm of it. CITRINE is on the other side of the throne, still fiddling with her cube. More than ever, she's ignored.)

Rose: Over the hill? Who says I'm over the hill?

Smokie: Nobody's saying you're over the hill, Rose. None of us are.

Amy: Not saying it, and certainly not over it!

. . .

CITRINE: What's that you say? Which hill, and where? There are far too many hills out beyond.

CHRYSSIE: I'm suggesting you look at <u>moving</u> over the hill.

ROSE: Moving? At our time of life?

SMOKIE: Moving isn't something we've ever been good at.

AMY: Not enthusiastic about, at any rate.

ROSE: Oh, I like moving. I can watch it for hours.

SMOKIE: If I get the urge to move, I sit quietly for a while until it passes.

AMY: Passes, yes. A movement is something humans do with their bowels, isn't it?

ROSE: I do not wish to know about that.

SMOKIE: What I wish to know about is why we'd even consider moving?

AMY: Moving away, over the hill.

. . .

CHRYSSIE: For your own good. *(SISTERS look puzzled.)* Your own safety. The lower caverns are getting restless. Someone's been stirring up trouble.

CITRINE: Trouble? Trouble? Toil and trouble,
   Fire burn and cauldron simmer.
   When there's someone stirs the pot
   Tis often 'cause they want the whole thing.

ROSE: Yes, well, we know who, don't we?

SMOKIE: That halfling boy of yours.

AMY: 'BOULDER' he calls himself now, and getting bolder by the week.

ROSE: He's got a silver tongue, that one.

SMOKIE: He could convince a lead ball it was a gold nugget!

AMY: He could unfasten a seam of copper!

CITRINE: Who...?

ROSE: But Ferrous will protect us.

. . .

CHRYSSIE: I doubt it. I doubt the king could protect <u>himself</u>, even if he saw a threat.

SMOKIE: It's true – our brother's not the troll he was.

AMY: I think the brat has been in his ear too. Undermining his self-confidence.

CITRINE: What?

ROSE: He's good at undermining.

SMOKIE: That's the troll side of him.

AMY: But he's undermining <u>us</u>.

CHRYSSIE: That's his other side. My fault, I know. A moment of girlish weakness.

CITRINE: When...?

ROSE: For which we're all now paying.

. . .

CHRYSSIE: Yes, all of us. Me included.

CITRINE: Where?

SMOKIE: He's got no loyalty to his family.

CHRYSSIE: He's got no loyalty to anyone.

CITRINE: How...?

AMY: Except to himself. That's the troll side of him. His mother's influence.

CITRINE: *(shuffling forward)* I'm old and deaf, not unaware!
    I'm treated as if not even there.
    For my thoughts, or questions they don't care -
    Such behaviour I'll no longer bear.
    My grand-daughters will no longer heed,
    Nor grandson try to intercede.
    If old Citrine you do not need
    Then that's how it shall be indeed.
    (CITRINE *puts down the cube and exits, passing un-noticed past everyone. "Rock of Ages" plays softly.*)

ROSE: Now listen, young Chrysoprase...

CHRYSSIE: Jade, now. I prefer that. It sounds... richer.

. . .

SMOKIE: What? Is changing names a new craze? Whatever next?

CHRYSSIE: Actually, that would be "Your Maj-" oh, never mind.

AMY: What was that?

CHRYSSIE: Never mind. It'd never sound sincere coming from you three anyway. Just, think about what I said, please. For your own sakes'.

(CHRYSSIE STARTS TO EXIT, *and meets SANDY coming in, out of earshot of the SISTERS.*)

CHRYSSIE: Ah, good – I wanted to see you.

SANDY: Here I am, Chryssie.

CHRYSSIE: Yes. Remember: I no longer wish to be called Chrysoprase. You are to call me Jade. Or better yet, Your Majesty.

SANDY: Your Majesty? Really? We've been friends for how long? You've always been Chryssie to me, ever since we were barely more than pebbles.

. . .

CHRYSSIE: Perhaps so. But now I'm going to take the throne.

SANDY: You've always been going to take the throne. Tradition or none. You're the king's daughter. Why is now different?

CHRYSSIE: I demand the proper respect due to a ruler.

SANDY: You have the respect due to my oldest friend.

CHRYSSIE: That is no longer – enough. And another thing. I need a new dress.

SANDY: Another? You need another?

CHRYSSIE: Want. It's the same thing. And I want silk. A darker shade than the last one.

SANDY: I don't have the fabric.

CHRYSSIE: You're my attendant, Sandy. Attend to finding some.

SANDY: I can ask Ch- Sir Chalk – to bring some back from Henriksberg.

. . .

CHRYSSIE: Can I trust the Fool to select the right shade to bring out the best in my delicate colouration? You should go.

SANDY: You're asking me to go out into a village-full of men?

CHRYSSIE: No. I'm telling you. I want that silk.

SANDY: Alright. I'll do what I can.

CHRYSSIE: Make it so. *(Exits.)*

SANDY: I swear she's getting worse. *(Picks up CITRINE's cube)* Oh - she's worked it out at last. Hmm – I wonder if the sisters have any silk? Greetings, ladies. Er – I just passed your grandmother. She appeared to be... going out?

ROSE: Out? Old Citrine never goes out.

SMOKIE: She hasn't passed through that portal since we were pebbles!

AMY: No, she's right over there, look... oh!

ROSE: I'd have sworn she was...

SMOKIE: Out, you say? How odd, even for her.

. . .

AMY: Well, she's certainly old enough to know her own mind.

SANDY: I suppose that's true. I hope she's okay. Dear ladies, I have a problem that I was hoping you might be able to help with.

ROSE: We shall, of course try.

SMOKIE: It's our very nature to be helpful.

AMY: Supportive.

ROSE: Sincere.

SMOKIE: Sensitive.

SANDY: Splendid, thank you. Chr... Ja... er, the king's daughter, has asked me to make her a new dress.

ROSE: Another?

SANDY: Afraid so.

SMOKIE: Ridiculous!

. . .

SANDY: Regrettable.

AMY: Unnecessary!

SANDY: Unavoidable – for me anyway. Do any of you have a quantity of dark green silk?

ROSE: We set no store by material wealth.

SMOKIE: Actually, we do. But we don't have much of it.

AMY: Less than we'd like, and the stocks are getting lesser.

ROSE: Green is not the colour for any of us. What we have, you may take. We have no argument with you, Sandy.

SANDY: Thank you, Rose.

SMOKIE: Come to our room later. No need for you to bear the brunt of all – that one's whims and fancies.

SANDY: I usually do. But I appreciate that, Smokie.

. . .

AMY: We should be packing and disposing of certain things, now that it's time for us to move on.

SANDY: You three? Move on? Where on earth to?

ALL THREE: Over the hill.

SANDY: Whose idea was that? Oh, wait. *(Looks in the direction where CHRYSSIE exited.)* I can guess.

ROSE: We make up our own minds.

SMOKIE: We are independent thinkers.

AMY: Yes, all three of us.

SANDY: But, after all this time here – where would you go?

ROSE: We have family.

SMOKIE: Our line goes far and wide.

AMY: Deep, if not rich.

. . .

Rose: <u>We</u> could take up sewing.

Smokie: Seriously? Us? Sewing what? Wild oats?

Rose: Hardly. Not at our time of life.

Amy: Sowing the seeds of discontent.

Rose: Sow discord.

Smokie: Sow dissatisfaction.

Amy: Sow disharmony.

Sandy: So like you. You'd soon wear out whatever welcome you got.

Rose: Sad but true. We could write our memoirs. The interesting story of our lives.

Smokie: A short story, then.

Amy: We'll write slowly.

(KING FERROUS ENTERS. *Theme music cuts off early.*)

. . .

KING: Hail to thee, young girl-troll, or troll-girl.
    I know your face, alas, your name's a-whirl.
    And hail to thee, my three dear siblings!
    What's this I hear you say of scribblings?

ROSE: We've decided to write our memoirs down,

SMOKIE: For posterity, and our renown.

AMY: It's important that our name endures,

ROSE: Not just as footnotes, stuck to yours.

SMOKIE: We have led our own lives, you know.

AMY: And we shall keep doing so.

KING: Of course, of course, my sisters dear!
    Those lives I've valued by me here.

ROSE: Hmph – that value placed, that once was high
    Has diminished as the time's gone by.

SMOKIE: We, who once led lives enchanted

Now are taken but for granted.

AMY: We were second, only just, to you,
    But the court has dwindled, and our status, too.

KING: Your words do leave me sore confused –
    Have I ever you abused?

ROSE: Abused us, no, but oft ignored,
    While your daughter wailed and roared.

SMOKIE: When we rightly should have your attention,
    Chrysoprase was all you'd mention.

AMY: Meanwhile court and retinue have shrunk.
    Our whole reputation's nearly sunk.

KING: Reputation? Retinue?
    Do my ears now do me true?
    Since when do such small things matter
    To trolls who can make mountains shatter?
    Our power and our traditions great...

ROSE: Are here outmoded, second-rate!

SMOKIE: How long since we moved the earth?
    Or showed the humans our true worth?

. . .

Amy: Once they knew respect, and fear.
    Now we're ghosts and legends living near.

King: We've never needed their regard.

Rose: Not 'needed', but its loss is hard.

Smokie: You, who talk of proud tradition

Amy: Have led us to a sad position.

King: I know not whence these words do spring.
    I've ne'er considered such a thing.
    I've said before that times are tough
    But always felt, enough's enough.
    These halls are not exactly poor –
    Tis strange to me you're wanting more.
    You're all still high in my esteem.
    My daughter now, I know does seem
    To be putting on some airs and graces
    But she's young, and the young don't know their places.

Rose: Oh, she knows the place to call her own.
    She wants to occupy the throne.

King: Sister Rose, don't tell such tales.

That seat may only pass to males.

Smokie: A tradition that she'll overthrow
       When to final slumber-land you go.

King: Be quiet! I will not hear such speech!

Amy: You must! Her grasp exceeds her reach.
     And we will not in silence bide
     To watch our stations further slide.

Rose: As Rose I should be loved and cherished
      But in this court my prestige's perished.

Smokie: Once this Smoke was well respected –
        Now I only feel neglected.

Amy: As sure as my name's Amethyst,
     Our treatment now gives me the schist.

Rose: Between your sloth, and her disdain
      Our pride we cannot now retain.

Smokie: The reasoning we've made quite plain.
        You cannot try now to complain.

. . .

AMY: Ferrous, get this through your brain:
   In this court we'll not remain!

KING: But...

ROSE: No!!

SMOKIE: No!

AMY: No.

SISTERS: No!!!

KING: I... understand. Well, no I don't. I only wonder...
   Your leaving... leaves me much to ponder. *(Exits, slowly, with no fanfare.)*

SANDY: Wow! That's something I never thought I'd see!

ROSE: Well, that's done it.

SMOKIE: The decision's been made.

AMY: And acted on.

. . .

Rose: Neither of which, admittedly, are things we've done a lot of, over the years.

Smokie: It's time we did more of both, then, if we're to be treated with the respect we deserve.

Amy: Firm decisions, yes, and decisive actions, are what we require if we're to establish ourselves properly wherever we might go.

Sandy: Might go? There's some chance you'll reconsider?

All three: No.

Rose: You must appreciate, Sandy, one thing we will not do, is change our minds once they're made up.

Smokie: We're not stubborn, you understand. Just determined.

Amy: What we must do now, though, sisters, is decide where we should grace with our presence.

Rose: Somewhere pleasant, with a view. Somewhere warm, perhaps.

Smokie: But not sunny. With <u>natural</u> light, to bring out our best colours.

. . .

Amy: Nothing beats the glow of volcanic light. We could relocate to the Costa Lava.

Rose: I believe Pumice is in charge there.

Smokie: Pumice? He's a lightweight! Would crumble under pressure.

Amy: He can be abrasive, though.

Rose: Still, never underestimate anyone who can get to the top.

Smokie: No matter how they get there.

Amy: Pumice has Basalt under him, remember, and she is <u>hard</u>!

All three: We remember!

Rose: Diplomacy, then.

Smokie: We can do that.

Amy: Yes. That and bribery. I don't believe they have our gold resources.

. . .

SANDY: I'm not sure that we do, any more.

ROSE: That's possible, you know. I think Chrysoprase, or Jade or whatever she wants to call herself, has been draining them for years.

SMOKIE: Yes, what with Ferrous never standing up to her whims and fancies.

AMY: And now being able to indulge herself.

ROSE: She'd never go to the lower caverns, surely?

SANDY: She doesn't have to.

SMOKIE: That's right. She'll send Cliff to throw his weight around.

SANDY: He enjoys that, I'm afraid. No wonder miners are getting fed up and starting to quietly leave.

AMY: All the more reason for us to take our leave, then, I think.

SISTERS: So say we all!

ROSE: I'll consult Sir Chalk on the quickest, safest route to the Costa Lava.

. . .

SMOKIE: I'll see what may yet be extracted from the treasury coffers.

AMY: I'll acquire some lower level trolls as retainers. We can't be expected to carry our own baggage.

SANDY: *(quietly)* You three will always carry baggage...

ROSE: Not too smart, mind, or too big. Nothing potentially dangerous to us.

SMOKIE: Nor too stupid, or too small. They must still be useful to us.

AMY: They must be just right. Or at least, just enough.

(SISTERS EXIT.)

SANDY: Honestly, I don't know whether to laugh, or cry.

BLACKOUT
   (Music fragment: "here we are and here we go, rockin' all over the world".)

ACT 2, SCENE 5

2:5

(LIGHTS UP.
　Music fragment: "Rock & Roll Part 1."
　CHRYSSIE and BOULDER pace, criss-crossing. CLIFF sits at the edge of the dais.)

BOULDER: Honestly, I'm amazed at how... intransigent he is. He's more rusted on than he ever was! With his sisters and grandmother gone, he's really dug in, which we didn't expect.

CHRYSSIE: He was supposed to lose heart.

BOULDER: Instead, he's found some spine.

. . .

CHRYSSIE: I thought you said he didn't want to rule any longer.

BOULDER: That was the impression he gave earlier. Maybe he's forgotten he ever said that.

CHRYSSIE: His mind is definitely wandering. He's becoming a danger to himself, and to the kingdom.

BOULDER: There's no higher authority to complain to.

CLIFF: Any complaints are supposed to go to the king.

BOULDER: We can't complain to the king about the king!

CLIFF: I suppose he's not likely to do anything about it if we did.

CHRYSSIE: He'd probably do something to you.

CLIFF: But I've been the royal guard for ages.

BOULDER: And when did he last thank you for your service?

CLIFF: Thank...? No-one ever thanks me.

. . .

CHRYSSIE: Anyway, more importantly, he doesn't want to give up the throne. Can't he see he isn't up to the job any more?

BOULDER: No, he can't. He can't even see, or remember, that there's any problems.

CLIFF: Um... what problems?

CHRYSSIE: That I want to take over the throne, for one thing!

BOULDER: Well, yes, but there are more, deeper ones.

CHRYSSIE: Not as far as I'm concerned.

BOULDER: You should be. Do you know that the treasury is almost empty?

CHRYSSIE: How did that happen?

CLIFF: Well...

CHRYSSIE: I'm not asking you! It was my aunts, I'll bet! Yes! Typical – even when they've gone, they manage to cause me grief. Empty. You're sure?

. . .

BOULDER: Almost empty. There's some gold left, and some gemstones, but not enough to be able to trade for supplies for very long. Although, saying that...

CHRYSSIE: What else?

BOULDER: There's not the same need for stuff here that there used to be. So many of the trolls below have left. Then again, it means that there are a lot less to do the work of extracting the jewels and such.

CHRYSSIE: If my father can turn things around, then so can I.

BOULDER: Do you really think he can? Me, I doubt it. Soon there won't be anyone left here to reign over. I understand you're ambitious, but who wants to be queen of a disintegrating society?

CHRYSSIE: I do.

BOULDER: Why?

CHRYSSIE: So that I will be important.

BOULDER: Mother, a – woman – like you can be important anywhere.

. . .

CHRYSSIE: Now you do sound like your father.

BOULDER: In that world out there, you really can be Jade. No-one there will know any better.

CLIFF: But Chrysoprase isn't really jade.

BOULDER: Most of <u>them</u> don't know the difference.

CHRYSSIE: Do you seriously expect that I can just go out amongst humans and rule?

BOULDER: Not rule – they don't work that way. But you can be successful, wealthy, popular, <u>important</u>. That's what you really want, isn't it?

CHRYSSIE: Well, yes. It won't be easy, of course.

CLIFF: I'll help.

CHRYSSIE: *(about to be dismissive, but pauses for a moment.)* Thank you, Cliff. I'll instruct the Fool to teach me all he knows of life out there. Go and get him. *(CLIFF exits.)* Obviously, I know quite a lot already.

BOULDER: Do you? Well, anyway, there's a lot you'll figure out as you go along. Money, negotiating, that sort of thing.

. . .

CHRYSSIE: I never negotiate.

BOULDER: You might have to, at first. They don't all understand the privileges of royalty.

CHRYSSIE: Well, they should. I'll soon teach them, with Cliff's help.

BOULDER: I really think you'll have more success with them if you understand something of human ways. *(CLIFF enters with CHALKIE, who has a newspaper under his arm.)* You understand what's expected of you?

CHALKIE: To a small extent. I'm to teach these two about life in the human world? All about it?

CHRYSSIE: Enough to get by, while we establish ourselves.

BOULDER: A basic survival course.

CHALKIE: Like you never had.

BOULDER: That's correct.

. . .

CHALKIE: Mind you, they're more set in their troll ways than you were as a child.

BOULDER: Start with something simple. Casual chat. A game, even.

CHALKIE: *(sighs)* Okay, I'll try. Humans do a lot of what they call 'small talk'.

CHRYSSIE: Why?

BOULDER: Because they've got small minds. *(He turns away, listening without being obvious about it.)*

CHALKIE: Some do, yes. But remember, they have much shorter lives than us. I don't think they realize that, as such, but long silences make many of them uncomfortable, so they fill the spaces with 'small talk'.

CHRYSSIE: They talk about small things.

CLIFF: Like pebbles, or mice, or blobs of bird poo...?

CHALKIE: Not exactly, but things of no real importance to them. Animals – are you a dog lover or a cat fancier?

CLIFF: I'll eat either.

. . .

CHALKIE: Or sport. Any sport. What team do you follow?

CHRYSSIE: Any team that wears green.

CHALKIE: Well, there are worse ways to decide. Or the weather – they talk a lot about the weather.

CHRYSSIE: Why? They don't erode.

CHALKIE: I know. It's strange, I admit. For something that they can't do anything about, humans do spend a lot of time complaining about the weather.

CHRYSSIE: I don't understand this idea of small talk. I only talk about what's important.

CHALKIE: Mostly you talk about yourself.

CLIFF: That's right.

CHALKIE: *(sighs again)* Okay. Let's try something else. This is a game called rock-paper-scissors…

(*THE THREE TROLLS go into a huddle. CHALKIE can be seen explaining rock-paper-scissors, to much confusion and incorrect hand movements over the following.*)

. . .

BOULDER: *(to himself.)* Another one bites the dust. My way is clear. Oh, it'll take time, I know that. I'm not worried. I'm patient. Trolls are born to patience, and I was born to a troll. But my patience isn't unlimited – that's something to be blamed on my father. My mother on the other hand, what she can be blamed for is being in my way. We both want the same thing, but only one of us will fit in that chair. It's a good thing that she's easily distracted. Both her, and her oversized lapdog. Distracted, and diverted.

(BY NOW, CHRYSSIE and CLIFF are playing rock-paper-scissors, CHALKIE sits apart, reading newspaper. BOULDER watches them all thoughtfully.)

CHRYSSIE: Rock.

CLIFF: Me too.

CHRYSSIE: Again. Silly game.

CHALKIE: Out there, rock beats scissors, but paper beats rock.

CLIFF: You got paper? *(CHALKIE holds out a sheet. CLIFF punches a hole in it.)* Stupid games these humans play. Me, I never read paper.

CHALKIE: No, I know that, Cliff.

. . .

BOULDER: What is that paper, anyway?

CHALKIE: Latest issue of 'The Gem'. News from other parts of the troll world, mostly.

BOULDER: We have enough trouble with this part of it! You don't need me to learn about – out there. Been there, done that, didn't like it. Chalk is more useful to you. He's more sympathetic. *(Exits angrily.)*

CHALKIE: Hard to be less sympathetic than your son. I'm surprised he's being so concerned about you and Cliff.

CHRYSSIE: He's frustrated with my father. I understand that. The difference is that Boulder is prepared to wait. I no longer am. I know better than he does how long trolls live. How long King Ferrous is likely to last.

CHALKIE: That's true. He's had a long reign already. There's no reason it shouldn't last a lot longer.

CHRYSSIE: There are plenty of reasons. But Ferrous won't listen to any of them. That's why it's time for me to leave.

CLIFF: Me too. What about you?

CHALKIE: I still have my loyalty to the king. It's different for me. It's my job.

. . .

CLIFF: Yeah. Fool.

CHRYSSIE: Elsewhere. Is there news we should know about?

CHALKIE: The troll press is taking an interest in – his father. Turns up a lot in 'Prospects and Pannings', too.

CHRYSSIE: What? Why?

CHALKIE: A scandalous celebrity. Newspapers love that.

CHRYSSIE: I can't imagine why. *(Pause.)* What's he up to?

CHALKIE: Exporting. After making good money selling idols to China, he's now turning a profit delivering missionaries there to convert the idol-worshippers.

CLIFF: Humans, huh, don't make sense.

CHALKIE: There are a lot of things you'll find – different, if you're determined to go out there. You <u>are</u> determined?

CLIFF: Er...

. . .

CHRYSSIE: I certainly am. It's about time I broadened my horizons. I'm worthy of more than what's available here.

CHALKIE: I thought you had an ambition to take over the throne. To become our first queen.

CHRYSSIE: What would be the point of being queen of a disintegrating realm? There was a time when this kingdom was rich, but not any longer.

CLIFF: I can't beat any more out of them miners, not that there's many left now. It's not like I can dig out gems and stuff myself.

CHALKIE: Actually, you probably could, you know. You're strong enough.

CHRYSSIE: That's true.

CLIFF: I wouldn't know where to start.

CHALKIE: Fair point. It's a job that requires experience, or at least training. Of those miners left, who'd be willing to take that on?

CHRYSSIE: I could order someone to do it.

CHALKIE: Theoretically, yes. How popular are you? Or Cliff?

. . .

CHRYSSIE: Popular? What does that have to do with anything?

CHALKIE: Cliff, what do you know about mineralogy?

CLIFF: Doesn't he live a couple of hills over to the west? Short troll, bad eyesight and a limp.

CHALKIE: My point is, Cliff would have to be trained by someone, to know what he's looking for. By someone who really knows, and would be willing to teach him properly. Someone he hasn't bullied or threatened.

CHRYSSIE: I... see...

CHALKIE: Without knowing better, he could spend hours, days, weeks even, loading himself up with nothing but worthless pyrite.

CLIFF: Who?

CHALKIE: No value at all. Do you know what humans call it? Fools gold. Not what you want to be known for, I should think.

CHRYSSIE: Indeed not. Well, I'll make sure we don't leave empty handed, but I do expect to become known for my strength of personality.

. . .

CLIFF: I'm just going to be known for my strength.

CHALKIE: For your sakes, I hope that's enough for both of you.

CHRYSSIE: Of course it will be.

(CHRYSSIE AND CLIFF EXIT, CLIFF still making 'rock' gestures. CHALKIE sits and reads the remaining bit of his paper. SANDY enters, looking over her shoulder in puzzlement.)

SANDY: That was unexpected! Chryssie and Cliff just rushed past me – they don't rush anywhere! I asked if there was anything I could do to help, and Cliff said, 'No' and that I was to look after myself.

CHALKIE: Unusually sound advice. What about 'Her Majesty'?

SANDY: She waved me away and said that they were going to help themselves.

CHALKIE: I can believe that.

SANDY: Then they kept hurrying off, without a backward glance.

. . .

CHALKIE: She doesn't let the grass grow under her, does she? Not any more. Not like poor old Citrine.

SANDY: What do you mean?

CHALKIE: I found her out on the hillside, in a sunny spot in a clearing. Just standing. Not moving.

SANDY: Oh no...

CHALKIE: She makes an attractive standing stone. Not very big, mind you. I doubt anyone will go so far as to worship her.

SANDY: I hope no humans smash her up for... building material.

CHALKIE: Unlikely. When we trolls set, whatever we <u>were</u> like, we usually become too hard to be broken up easily. As I say, though, she's quite small. I could see her becoming part of a building. A lintel over a doorway, maybe.

SANDY: She often did go over the heads of those around her.

CHALKIE: *(after a pause)* Did Chryssie talk with you about her – plans for you and her son?

. . .

SANDY: Earlier, yes. Not with me, but to me. I was directed to deflect his attention from the throne 'by whatever means necessary'. When I asked what that was supposed to mean, she said I was to seduce him, then distract him with a family. Produce a child any time he looked to be taking any interest in kingship.

CHALKIE: That's even less subtle than I expected! What did you say?

SANDY: No.

CHALKIE: Brave. Understandable, though.

SANDY: For a start, while I know what seduction is, I'm afraid it would come as naturally to me as floating. Secondly, if I did decide to learn, he is not my idea of a desirable mate. I said 'no' to his father a long time ago, and the son is a good deal less appealing. I'm not opposed to the idea of being a mother, but I think it should be my decision, not the subject of 'royal decree'.

CHALKIE: I'm disappointed in Chryssie. I really thought she put a higher value on your friendship. I suppose that's why I'm officially the court Fool.

SANDY: Don't be hard on yourself, Chalkie. I thought better of her, too, for a long time. She's changed. Become harder, slowly but surely, ever since that business with Peer.

CHALKIE: How did she take your saying "no"?

. . .

SANDY: As well as you'd expect. It's not a word she's familiar with.

CHALKIE: Oh, she knows the word well. She's used to saying it, just not hearing it.

SANDY: That's right. Stamped her foot, waved her fists, even threatened to have Cliff 'deal with me', whatever that's supposed to mean. Cliff's not very bright, but he's not really nasty.

CHALKIE: But you stood your ground.

SANDY: Let's just say, I don't think I'll be a 'royal attendant' for much longer. It's just a matter of whether I jump before I'm pushed.

CHALKIE: I don't think you need to worry. I wonder if your little act of defiance was a final push for her? One change too many for her ego? Ah, well. Good luck to the outside world.

SANDY: Tell me about this rock music.

CHALKIE: I DO LIKE HUMANS' rock music. A nice change from the music of rocks we get here, that Boulder could never really rise above. My favourite band is, of course, the Rolling Stones. I've often wondered if there's a bit of troll in Keith Richards.

. . .

SANDY: Not this Mick Jagger I've heard about?

CHALKIE: I'd be more inclined to believe there's been a bit of Mick Jagger in in a troll or two. Seriously, though, Sandy - I think you could make a go of living in the outside world, if that's what you want.

SANDY: Not so much what I want, but what is there for me here? With 'Her Majesty' leaving, that's the end of my days as a 'royal attendant'. King Ferrous has never wanted or needed anyone beyond you, and I'm certainly not going to do the same sort of job for the brat as a career.

CHALKIE: Another meaning of career is to plummet uncontrollably downward. That's an easy thing for a careless troll to do, but I don't think that you're careless. If your facial markings cause you trouble, a little make-up can fix it. That's worked on me for years, and as a female it'd be even less conspicuous on you.

SANDY: Thanks for the tip. But Chalkie, what could I do? It's not like I can sing the way Chip – Boulder – did.

CHALKIE: Not many sing the way 'Iggy Coaldust' did, for which the music industry can be deeply grateful.

SANDY: He said he could sing.

CHALKIE: He's said, and continues to say, a lot of things. I'm afraid our young would-be ruler is a stranger to the truth, when it suits him.

. . .

SANDY: He says he doesn't want to be king... oh, I see. Another untruth?

CHALKIE: Not a lie, but a technicality. He doesn't want the title of "king", so it is true, in its way. But he does want his grandfather's authority. It's the same with his singing, I suppose. He probably does believe he can sing.

SANDY: Others disagree?

CHALKIE: The ones who've heard him. He couldn't carry a tune in a coal scuttle.

SANDY: I guess I'm not <u>that</u> bad...

CHALKIE: If you've got no confidence in yourself, it's not a profession I'd recommend, I'm sorry.

SANDY: Thanks. I don't think dancing is an option for a troll in the land of light.

CHALKIE: There is a thing called 'slow dancing', but I don't think it's something to try to make a living from if you want to preserve your dignity.

. . .

SANDY: That would be my preference.

CHALKIE: Some trolls have become fighters, of various sorts, over the years.

SANDY: No.

CHALKIE: No, I agree. Hmm – we talked before about your not being careless. It prompts me to think: there's a job in human society called a 'professional carer'.

SANDY: You're kidding!

CHALKIE: A strange concept to a troll, I know. It requires someone who's a good listener, sympathetic, but knows how to be hard when the situation requires it.

SANDY: I can learn to do all that.

CHALKIE: Sandy, you already know. And as a troll, you already possess one of the most essential attributes a professional carer can have – a very thick skin.

SANDY: It sounds plausible, if not exactly attractive.

CHALKIE: Maybe worth a try.

. . .

SANDY: I wouldn't know where to start.

CHALKIE: <u>Not</u> Henriksberg. Perhaps old Peer had the right idea when he headed for the sea.

SANDY: I've never seen the sea.

CHALKIE: Big. Wet. Quite a good thing to be beside, for you and me. Not so good to be under.

SANDY: You and me?

CHALKIE: Purely platonic, of course. I'd like to help you find your feet.

SANDY: I know where my feet are. But I would appreciate some guidance on where to put them. What I should or shouldn't tread on.

CHALKIE: I'd be happy to do that. I do still owe service to the king, though. I can't just abandon him. Even – especially – when everyone else has.

SANDY: I admire your loyalty. I confess I've never been close to him. Chryssie was always... in the way.

. . .

CHALKIE: Ferrous has never been easy to be close to. By nature, and by choice.

SANDY: Aloof, like "Her Majesty Jade"?

CHALKIE: No, not aloof as such. I don't think he sees himself that way, at any rate. I don't think he sees himself at all, as such. It's all about the role, and traditions, of being king. Right down to the archaic speech pattern. He doesn't do that consciously, you know. It's a very long-etched habit.

SANDY: You'll stay with him, as long as… required.

CHALKIE: I'm afraid so. I <u>want</u> to help you. Be a mentor, a guide…

SANDY: And I appreciate that. I'll wait, keep my head down. The lower regions trolls have mostly quietly left. Gone west to work in mines where the rewards are greater and conditions better.

CHALKIE: Do we still have a bit of treasure? Some gold reserve? *(SANDY shakes her head.)* I know how Chip – Iggy – Boulder, financed his extended stay in the world outside. How he afforded the 'rock star' lifestyle he tried.

SANDY: Then Rose, Smokie and Amy made sure they wouldn't do without. No begging for them, nor working.

. . .

CHALKIE: AND OF COURSE, WITH 'JADE' convinced to go and make her mark, she'll need something to make it with.

SANDY: I think that's where she and Cliff were headed when I saw them. Maybe I can slip out and down the hill now and then, to... check things out. Acclimatise to the conditions.

CHALKIE: That might be wise. You might even find you like Henriksberg.

SANDY: Unlikely, from what I do already know. Especially if Chryssie and Cliff get settled in.

CHALKIE: I doubt that. I expect it won't take long for them to leave, by choice or by force.

SANDY: Humans couldn't really hurt a troll, could they?

CHALKIE: One on one, it would be difficult, but an angry mob is different. Pitchforks and flaming torches don't mean a lot to us beyond some eye pain, but some well-placed sledgehammers can hurt. Even someone Cliff's size.

SANDY: If I know Chryssie, whatever gold and gems she takes won't last long. She has no idea of budgeting. Never had to.

· · ·

CHALKIE: Cliff would be no better. No head for treasure, except for smashing it out of a cave wall. And when their money's gone, so too will be any minor celebrity or attraction they may have had.

SANDY: You're cynical about how fickle humans are.

CHALKIE: Yes. About 'CELEBRITY' especially. Money, less so, but even that's no guarantee of popularity.

SANDY: You did warn them?

CHALKIE: I tried. How much got through, I'm not sure. Not a lot, I'm afraid.

SANDY: You tried, Chalkie. That will have to be enough.

BLACKOUT
(Music fragment: "We're stepping out, gonna turn around once and do the eagle rock".)

ACT 2, SCENE 6

2:6

(LIGHTS UP: KING *is in his throne.*
 BOULDER *is striding around in front of him, arrogantly.*
 CHALKIE *and* SANDY *stand at a distance, any efforts to approach stopped by a gesture from the* KING.
 A few troll newspapers lie nearby.)

BOULDER: Soon, it'll be too late, if it isn't already. I've been out there. I've seen it, and I know! Trolls have become creatures out of mythology. Worse, figures of fun. Once, humans feared trolls, now they laugh at them. At us. At you. Their children used to be terrified of us. Now they make toy trolls to dangle over cots and hang off their mirrors.

. . .

CHALKIE: Unfortunately, that is true.

BOULDER: And this has happened under <u>your</u> reign. Trolls are no longer respected. No longer dangerous.

CHALKIE: Some still are.

SANDY: Inside here, especially.

BOULDER: If you truly wanted to do the right thing by trolls, all trolls, you'd have stepped aside long ago, instead of... fossilising. How long since you set your royal foot in the mines? Decades? More?

KING: For such duties, I've a court.
    Responsibilities were taught...

BOULDER: Oh yes, delegate. That's the way to avoid taking the blame yourself. Nothing could be <u>your</u> fault.

CHALKIE: A common refrain among the royal bloodline, it must be said.

BOULDER: Look around you. It's clear you're no longer fit to rule.

KING: What's all too clear is your position.
    To be the king is your ambition.

. . .

BOULDER: You're wrong, in this as in so much else. It's one thing to want to be in charge. To have authority. But I would not take the title of 'King". That's an anachronism. An old legend outside this hall, and soon enough, what everyone inside here will come to believe.

KING: You'd dare suggest there's no such thing
　　As the mountain hall's own noble king?
　　(CHALKIE and SANDY advance.)
　　Hold, friends, your defence un-needed
　　Such a one's not to be heeded.

BOULDER: No? There's your trouble right there. Not heeding advice. No wonder your sisters abandoned you. And your daughter, and your guard. You don't listen to anyone. It's no surprise you're treated as if you don't exist – it's all you deserve!

KING: But can you neither see nor hear?
　　Tis clear as mud that I'm still here.

BOULDER: You're a relic. A tramp. A wastrel and a waste. History will forget you, like you never existed.

KING: Your abuse then seems a pointless crime.
　　If I never existed, you're wasting your time.

BOULDER: You're right. *(Turns away. Ignores KING and converses only with CHALKIE and SANDY)*

. . .

SANDY: The king's done nothing...

BOULDER: Exactly. And see where that's gotten us all.

SANDY: Nothing wrong, I was about to say.

BOULDER: Nothing at all, more accurately.

KING: What would you do in my place,
    To bring respect back to our race?
    Grandson, I would speak more of this.
    My sisters' counsel, I do miss.
    Can our trolldom's ancient glory
    Be no more than bedtime story?

BOULDER: *(to CHALKIE)* You could try telling him. He won't listen to anyone else though – why would a Fool get through to him?

CHALKIE: Sire, I admit that there is a grain of truth in what he says, but...

KING: I command you to keep still, Sir Chalk.
    It needs be to this youth I talk.

. . .

BOULDER: Not my need. I've said all I had to say. To you, Fool, and to… the one who used to occupy that throne. *(BOULDER exits.)*

KING: My mind is in dark thoughts now mired.
   Perhaps it is time I retired.
   Follow in my Grandma's paces
   And take me to the sunlit places.
   No, Sir Chalk, I need no help
   To contemplate that crafty whelp.
   I see the game he tries at playing,
   But I see the truth that's underlaying.
   Has my time at this mountain's helm
   Been the ruin of the realm?

CHALKIE: No, sire! I…

(KING EXITS.)

SANDY: How does he do it? He's got poor Ferrous doubting himself. He got Rose, Smokie and Amy to abandon the hall. He even convinced Cliff and Chrysoprase that they can achieve some sort of greatness among humans!

CHALKIE: HE PLAYED ON THE SISTERS' vanity, just like he's playing on the king's true fears. As to the other two, Boulder just told them what they wanted to hear. The truth is, Cliff will fit in like a bowling ball into a sock. Chryssie will stand out like a cucumber in a bowl of custard.

. . .

SANDY: She won Peer over, remember.

CHALKIE: Briefly. And frankly, Peer was never the finest example of mankind. Nor always the most – discerning. He does get around, mind you, even now. I found a copy of an old "Lapis Leisurely" out of Africa. It seems Peer found his way into one of the desert kingdoms there, and ran off with a local chieftain's daughter. Or she ran off with him.

SANDY: That does sound familiar. Did they live happily ever after?

CHALKIE: Of course not, although the paper is rather coy about who left who. Probably neither was what the other expected.

SANDY: He hasn't changed, has he?

CHALKIE: Yet, I used to hear all the time out there: "people change'. I always thought that was one of the great differences between us and them. That, for better or for worse, trolls don't change. But I look around now...

SANDY: Do you consider growing older 'change'?

CHALKIE: Not necessarily. Growing wiser certainly is, though.

. . .

(THE KING, *without his robe or a fanfare, enters sits heavily on the dias in front of the throne, his head resting on his staff, which is now clearly only a stick. CHALKIE and SANDY approach cautiously.*)

CHALKIE: Your Majesty?

KING: My majesty now is a thing in tatters.
    Not head nor heart for regal matters.

SANDY: Sire, what's the source of this despair?

CHALKIE: I have a fair idea…

KING: Yes, faithful Chalk. I'm sure you guess
    The origin of my distress.
    There's no-one left beneath our feet,
    The miners' path, an empty street.
    My whole existence I now doubt –
    Have I let my kingdom's sands run out?
    Should I have kept a firmer hand –
    Tried changing times to understand?

SANDY: You've done your best. Surely that's…

KING: My best, it seems, has little worth
    When all about me turns to earth.

. . .

CHALKIE: It's always been earth. We're trolls, it's what we are.

KING: We valued high our seeing double,
    Finding grandeur in the rubble.
    But now I find that vision fades.
    What once was glory, now degrades.
    The trolls who lived below have left,
    Of followers I'm now bereft.
    All our treasure could not save.
    This palace now is but a cave.

SANDY: It's sad, but it's hard to argue.

CHALKIE: I've never argued with Ferrous, and I can't start now.

KING: My grandson tells me I'm a myth
    In the world beyond our monolith.
    Has he told the truth, or lied?
    I'll never know while here I bide.

SANDY: Does that matter?

CHALKIE: You're not a young troll, Ferrous. The conditions outside will not be – kind to you, you must know.

KING: It may be madness – this I know.
    But into the sunlight I must go.
    Of dangers, yes, I am aware,

But honestly, I do not care.
If all my life has been for nought
To lose it's scarcely worth a thought.

SANDY: It is to us, sire! Let us go with you. Help you, where and how we can.

CHALKIE: My place has ever, ultimately, been at your side.

KING: Such loyalty is appreciated,
And too often, I fear, under-rated. *(Shakes his head.)*
I thank you both, for all you've said
And done, to try to ease my head.
No. Even if the going's rough
To mine own self, I must be enough. *(Exits.)*
(Music fragment: "he was Too Old To Rock and Roll, but he was too young to die".)

SANDY: Where does that leave us?

CHALKIE: Alone.

SANDY: There's nothing for us – for you – here now.

CHALKIE: True. All too true. Time to depart, I think.

SANDY: I've already packed.

. . .

CHALKIE: Hah – same here! Not that there was much to pack. Little here, less in Henriksberg.

SANDY: We're still heading coastwards, aren't we?

CHALKIE: That's the plan, if I can call it that. We'll be living on our wits for a while, Sandy.

SANDY: We won't be travelling as light as some others, then. In a bag I've got some good fabric, needles and thread. They may help.

CHALKIE: They certainly should. I've seen your work. You should find some easier clients among humankind. Easier to fit, and easier to please. Some of them, at least.

SANDY: It's hard to imagine them being more challenging than 'Her Majesty'. Some may try, but I can take my business elsewhere if I want.

CHALKIE: Good attitude. I think you'll go far.

SANDY: We'll go far, and go together. Barring accidents, we should both live long lives, Chalkie, and I'd like to grow old with a good friend. Let's be on our way, shall we?

. . .

CHALKIE: Wait for me at the gate, my friend. I've one last official task to perform. My resignation.

SANDY: Is that really necessary? Do you think Boulder will care?

CHALKIE: No, but it's not for him to care about. It's for me. Closure. This job has been my life for, well, most of my life.

SANDY: Alright. I get it. I'll be waiting. *(Exits.)*

CHALKIE: Not for long, I hope. *(He pulls a newspaper from the little pile and sits, reading.)* I'd thought I might share some news with King Ferrous. Too bad. He may even find out for himself, I suppose. I wonder if he can read.

(BOULDER STRIDES IN, carrying KING's robe, with which he wipes the throne before he sits.)

BOULDER: And then there were none. *(He looks down his nose at CHALKIE.)* You're still here? Well, where else would you be, I suppose. You are the court historian, as well as Fool. And history certainly has been unfolding.

CHALKIE: It has. Here and beyond. Even in Henriksberg, or near to it.

BOULDER: No interest to me, or relevance to us.

. . .

CHALKIE: Oh, a bit. Your father is back.

BOULDER: You've been told to never mention his name!

CHALKIE: I didn't. Only his place in your – our – history.

BOULDER: That man is dead to me.

CHALKIE: He's only human. Before too long he really will be, and you won't have to worry about him any longer.

BOULDER: Whoever said that I was worried?

CHALKIE: There's an interesting story in 'The Tailings'. That hut where your mother found him years ago still stands, as does the love of the woman who still lives there. No, I don't understand it, either.

BOULDER: Meaningless to me.

CHALKIE: The emotion, or the news?

BOULDER: Either. Both.

. . .

CHALKIE: Of course. Most things are, or so you say. Amazing things, these humans. He was truly loved by <u>someone</u>, all this time. And ironically, all this time, to thine own self, you have been true.

BOULDER: *(menacingly)* Get out of here.

CHALKIE: With pleasure. *(Goes to exit. BOULDER has looked around at the empty room.)*

BOULDER: Wait! You've always been here for me. I've always been your friend.

CHALKIE: You've never been my friend. And while I've been, or tried to be, many things to you – jester, history teacher, advisor, a voice of reason – a lone voice all too often – I have never been your friend. I think I managed that with your father, sometimes, on those occasions when he realised that his Self wasn't enough for himself. You, however, have never even had that much self-awareness. You see, and point out, and mock, all the faults and inadequacies in others. But you've never seen any in yourself.

BOULDER: Are you saying I'm vain?

CHALKIE: You have more than a vein of quartz in you – you're a child of your mother's family. But no, you don't find fault in yourself, not because it isn't there, but because you've never looked. *(Tosses the paper at BOULDER's feet, then exits.)*

. . .

BOULDER: Faults. My faults. My fault. That Fool is a... a... a fool! I am right. I am the authority. Yes, I am the one in charge here now. The... one. And I am... enough.

(SFX CRICKETS)
BLACKOUT
(Music fragment: "And a rock feels no pain, and an island never cries.")

END

FROM THE PLAYWRIGHT...

Back in 1974, I appeared as a troll in a High School production of Henrik Ibsen's *Peer Gynt*. The show was so successful that we travelled from Brisbane to Canberra (about 1200 kilometres, or 745 miles, for those of you not familiar with Australian geography) to put on an additional performance.

That's a fair effort for a bunch of teenagers, and says as much for the play as it does for those involved. Certainly, it stuck with many of us for many years.

As a writer, I especially loved Ibsen's referencing of myth and legend - the weighing up and melting down of undeserving souls, the formless and sinister Boyg, and especially the trolls.

They're mostly met in one scene, with the consequences of Peer's time in the King's hall mentioned on several subsequent occasions. I've taken that scene, and those references, and fleshed them out to give the trolls the spotlight I think they deserve.

Where possible, I've used dialogue from Ibsen's play, in some instances modified to be a little more appropriate for my purposes.

My version of troll society mixes some Ibsen, some fairy tale, some Terry Pratchett, and some of my own imaginings.

Ibsen wanted to make some points about human nature - good points, I think - in the course of his story. I wanted to do the same, while making that story more contemporary, without losing its basis in fantasy.

I hope you'll agree that Henrik, and I, have achieved it. Enjoy!

HENRI RENNIE

NOTES FOR DIRECTORS

The Hall of the Mountain King is meant to be fun. Keep that in mind, and it should be hard to go wrong.

Be as extravagant, or as simple, with production as your heart desires, your imagination extends, and your budget allows. I do think that using colours as 'themes' for each of the characters gives you something to play with, as well as providing some visual appeal for the audience. And those colours should stand out well against a dull, mostly grey background.

If you have a good number of performers to work with, there is scope for 'crowd scenes', particularly in Act 1. Choreographing a court-full of trolls in Scenes 4, 5 and 6 could be entertaining.

The music was meant to be a key element in the humour of the play. For copyright reasons, I've suggested using only small fragments of some well-known rock songs. They're not integral to the story though, so please feel free to consider other options - including commissioning your own if you have some talented musicians in your group.

I do strongly suggest, though, that you use a good rendition of Grieg's *Hall of the Mountain King* from the *Peer Gynt Suite*, as the opening music at least. It's among the most instantly recognizable pieces of classical music, anywhere in the world.

To return to my first point: enjoy yourself with this script. If you, your cast, and crew, are having fun, your audience will too. Henrik Ibsen and I both want to provoke some thought in the watcher, but if they can learn while they're laughing, then we, and you, will have accomplished something special.

Best wishes.

HENRI

ALSO BY HENRI 'RENOIR' RENNIE

Find us at *www.meredian.com.au*

The DUBIOUS MAGIC series:

The Wizard of Waramanga

The Carvings of Cobbemarmoo

The Mad Machines of Mundara

The Warriors of Wiwo'ole

The Spirits of Sron Dubh

The Sailors of Svalgsay

The Treasure of Tepatamwa

The Masks of Manovalo

ALSO:

The Fall of DeWilde

The LOST Saga

He Was Beeb When I Knew Him

Mixed Blood

These Old Bastards...

The MEN'S HEALTH - A QUIET WORD Series

Mid-Life Crisis MANagement - Surviving Middle Age & Male Menopause

Move It Like You Mean It - A Quiet Word About Parkinsons Disease In Men

www.ingramcontent.com/pod-product-compliance
Lightning Source LLC
Chambersburg PA
CBHW051437290426
44109CB00016B/1587